WEB
OF
PUNISHMENT

An Investigation

Carol Coulter

Attic Press
Dublin

WEB
OF
PUNISHMENT

An Investigation

First published in Ireland in 1991 by
Attic Press
44 East Essex Street
Dublin 2

British Library Cataloguing in Publication Data
Coulter, Carol
    Web of punishment.
    1. Great Britain. Prisoners. Families
    I. Title
    362.8293

    ISBN 1-85594-022-1

Cover Design: Denise Kierans
Origination: Attic Press
Printing: The Guernsey Press Co Ltd

To the families of all Irish prisoners,
and especially those
serving sentences in Britain

Carol Coulter was born in Sligo and now works in Dublin for *The Irish Times*. She won the 1990 National Media Award for outstanding work in campaigning journalism for her coverage of the cases of the Birmingham Six and the Guildford Four.

Acknowledgements

This book could not have been written without the help of a great many people. Foremost among them are the prisoners and their families who took me into their confidence and gave generously of their time and hospitality. Sincere thanks to all of them. I will not name them individually only because those not already in the public eye may not welcome the attention this would bring.

I could not have met many of them without the help and cooperation of people working with them, who went to great lengths to find families across a broad spectrum of circumstances and, where necessary, quelled any doubts they might have had about talking to journalists. They also offered me the benefit of their own experience and research and were prepared to talk to me at length, discussing my observations and outlining conclusions they had come to. These include Tony Caffney of Sinn Féin, Lita Campbell of Republican Sinn Féin, Sister Sarah Clarke, Hester Dunne of Justice for Lifers, Father Denis Faul, Father Bobby Gilmore, Carol Horner and other staff of the Northern Ireland Association for the Care and Resettlement of Offenders, the press office of the Northern Ireland Office, Mrs Eleanor Hughes for access to the thesis of her late husband, the Reverend William James Hughes, Nuala Kelly of The Irish Commission for Prisoners Overseas, Jackie McArthur of the Bible Christian Centre Outreach to Prisoners, Gareth Peirce, solicitor, Marty Rafferty of the Quakers' family centres at Long Kesh and Maghaberry prisons, William Smith of Justice for All, and Mike Tomlinson of the Sociology Department of Queen's University, Belfast.

This book would not have been possible without the help of *The Irish Times*, which gave me time off to work on it, and the encouragement of the staff of Attic Press, starting with their initial persuasion and continuing with their readiness to help me solve problems as they arose.

Numerous friends and members of my family tolerated my talking about little other than what was happening to prisoners' families for some four months, and Harry Vince and John Daly read the manuscript and offered helpful criticism.

Contents

Preface

Covering the cases of the Birmingham Six and the Guildford Four for *The Irish Times* it was impossible to avoid seeing the suffering of the families of those wrongly convicted. However, in the public discussion of these cases their plight has received scant attention.

There have been a few exceptions. The film *Dear Sarah*, based on the experiences of Sarah Conlon, mother of Gerry Conlon of the Guildford Four and married to Giuseppe Conlon, and the recent BBC *Everyman* programme about the families of the Birmingham Six, showed that they, too, had been sentenced. The tragedy that engulfed their sons and husbands had also shattered their lives. But these films have not prompted any broader examination of the effects of imprisonment on the families.

Such films are damning indictments of the inhumanity of these systems, shown to be totally indifferent to the needs of the families of the convicted men, and in many instances actually vindictive. Nowhere has this vindictiveness been shown more sharply than in the adamant refusal of the Home Office in Britain to transfer these prisoners back to serve their sentences in Northern Ireland, closer to their families.

This problem is shared by the families of prisoners in Britain who have not proclaimed their innocence. Yet their families are innocent, no less so than the families of the Guildford Four and the Birmingham Six. They too are serving sentences involving great hardship and suffering as they struggle to maintain a relationship with their husband, father, son, brother or, more rarely, sister, daughter, mother, or wife who has fallen foul of the British legal system.

As I found out about these people, it was clear that they, the

11

families of Irish prisoners serving long sentences in Britain, were only an extreme example of a widespread phenomenon. They were the worst affected category of prisoners' family, but their envy of the situation of those whose loved one was serving a sentence in Long Kesh, Maghaberry, Magilligan or Armagh served only to underline the abnormality of the situation in the North of Ireland, where such a high proportion of the population has been affected by the experience not only of bereavement, but of imprisonment, over the past twenty years.

According to the Northern Ireland Office, which started keeping records in 1973, 14,220 people have been charged with a 'terrorist type' offence between 1973 and October 1990. On average, some 85 per cent of those charged are convicted, giving a figure of 12,087 convictions over the past seventeen years. This includes some individuals with more than one conviction.

In the society of the North, where in both nationalist and loyalist communities families are extended and family links are strong, parents, in-laws, brothers, mothers and sisters as well as wives will be affected by the imprisonment of a family member; one can conservatively guess at ten people involved per prisoner. Allowing that the number convicted includes those with more than one conviction and that in some families more than one person is convicted, we reach a figure of approximately 100,000 people in the North with direct experience of the effects of imprisonment during the past seventeen years. This does not include those jailed in Britain and in the Republic for politically-motivated offences over that period, most of whom, though by no means all, come from the North of Ireland.

The overwhelming majority of prisoners come from working class areas and from small farms. In the current troubles in the North of Ireland it is mainly the poor who go to jail and many of those who are killed are also poor. These are the very people whose voice is least heard in political institutions and in the media.

It would surely be foolish to imagine that the experience of such people, and the solutions, if any, which will be offered to prisoners in any proposed settlement of the conflict in the North, will have no bearing on the eventual outcome of the ongoing political crisis there. Yet the experiences of prisoners and their families are rarely mentioned publicly in any of the many discussions of the future of the North. In the first year of the Anglo-Irish Agreement there was some attempt to put the needs of prisoners' families on the agenda, and this was planned for the second year of its operations, according to sources close to the then coalition government. However, when that government was replaced by a Fianna Fáil government in February 1987 the problems of prisoners and their families were dropped.

At a purely humanitarian level there are thousands of people, women and children in the main, who are experiencing separation, stress, poverty and the disruption of their lives because of imprisonment. They have been charged with no crime, sentenced in no court, are innocent in the eyes of the law. Yet the law takes decisions which effectively punish them and which take no account of their needs.

In writing this book I spoke to over sixty people, ranging from politicians, social workers, priests, and people working for prisoners to ex-prisoners and members of prisoners' families. When quoting those who operate in the public domain, such as politicians, campaigners and those working with prisoners and their families, I use their full names, except where requested not to do so. I also use full names when describing the experiences of people whose cases have already entered the public domain, like the families of the Birmingham Six, the Guildford Four and the Winchester Three. However, when quoting prisoners and relatives whose lives have not been made public, and who trusted me with their experiences and their often very intimate feelings, I use only first names.

Where the experience of imprisonment is part of a tradition certain terms enter the language of those who undergo that experience. In the North this is combined with the language of the political tradition, and language itself becomes a field of battle. Many prisoners and their families refer to the prison officers as 'screws', and where they do so I quote them. All republican prisoners and many loyalists refer to the Maze prison by its original name, Long Kesh, and I follow this in the interests of clarity.

13

Notes

On Thursday 19 October 1989, Paddy Armstrong, Gerard Conlon and Carole Richardson of the Guildford Four were released from the Old Bailey when their convictions were quashed. The following day, 20 October 1989, Paul Hill was released on bail from the Appeal Court in Belfast.

On Thursday 14 March 1991, the convictions of the Birmingham Six were quashed and Hugh Callaghan, Paddy Joe Hill, Gerry Hunter, Richard McIlkenny, Billy Power and Johnny Walker were released from the Old Bailey in London.

Glossary

Brew Slang for unemployment and other social assistance

Category A The high security category given to prisoners in Britain convicted of very serious and 'terrorist-type' offences, involving very restrictive conditions for the prisoners and their visitors

Category B The category given to 'ordinary' prisoners, with less restrictive conditions

DHSS The Department of Health and Social Security, which grants unemployment assistance and other forms of social assistance

H-Blocks The section of the Maze Prison (Long Kesh) to which prisoners were moved when 'Special Category' (political) status was abolished

High Security Special units in certain prisons in Britain used for prisoners convicted of very serious offences

ICPO The Irish Commission for Prisoners Overseas, run by the Irish Bishops

IRA The Irish Republican Army (nationalist and drawn from the catholic community). The IRA split into the 'Provisionals' and 'Officials', the latter came to be known as 'Stickies' in local slang

Licence Life-sentenced and SOSP prisoners are released on parole after ten or more years (this is discretionary) with a 'licence' which specifies that parole may be revoked if, in the opinion of the police, they are in danger of reoffending

NACRO National Association for the Care and Resettlement of Offenders, a non-governmental agency

NIACRO Northern Ireland Association for the Care and Resettlement of Offenders, a non-governmental agency

NIO Northern Ireland Office, which administers Northern Ireland

PTA Prevention of Terrorism Act, introduced in Britain in 1973, which includes provision for holding people for questioning for seven days and deporting people to Northern Ireland or to the Republic

Screws Slang for prison warders

SOSP On the Secretary of State's Pleasure, the indefinite sentences served by those convicted of murder who were under eighteen at the time of the offence

Stickies see IRA

UDR The Ulster Defence Regiment, a regiment of the British Army recruited locally, mainly from the protestant community, to assistant the British Army and RUC (police)

UVF The Ulster Volunteer Force, loyalist and drawn from the protestant community

Introduction

There were 1,802 people in prison in Northern Ireland in March 1990, of whom 73 per cent were serving sentences ranging from four years to life imprisonment or sentences 'On the Secretary of State's Pleasure', the unlimited sentences served by those under eighteen when the crime was committed. In Northern Ireland 'lifers' make up a quarter of the prison population, compared with five per cent in England and Wales, seven per cent in Scotland and four per cent in the Republic of Ireland. Over half the prisoners were in prison for an offence involving 'violence against the person'. These statistics cover the majority of those convicted of politically-motivated crimes. Only three per cent of the prisoners were women.

This is a slight decline on the average prison population for 1989, which was 1,815, and that year in turn had seen a reduction of five per cent on the previous year, part of a general downward trend from the high point of some 3,000 in the late 1970s. Nonetheless the prison population in the North, relative to the overall population and especially compared to the figures for the period before the onset of the present troubles, remains high.

Previous Research on Prisoners' Families

Existing studies of the effects of imprisonment on the families of prisoners are few and far between and are aimed at social workers and other professionals in the area rather than the general public. Those which do exist deal with prisoners serving sentences of usually less than five years. Prisoners in Northern Ireland, and Irish prisoners in Britain, serve much longer sentences (in December 1990 two people were sentenced in

Britain to thirty years on conspiracy charges), and such sentences pose different problems for the families. But it can reasonably be assumed that they will share to a greater or lesser extent the problems of families who have relatives serving shorter sentences for 'ordinary' crimes to a greater or lesser extent.

The most important study on this subject, still widely quoted by academics and workers with prisoners and their families, remains Pauline Morris's *Prisoners and their Families*, published in 1965 and now out of print. She took a sample of 837 men, designed to be representative of the married prison population as a whole. Predictably, she found that imprisonment put great strain on marriages. Twenty five years ago, when divorce was much less common than it is now, one third of the sample reported broken marriages. Poverty was another problem for most of them. Four out of ten of the women saw money as their main problem, and seventy-eight per cent were in receipt of national assistance.

The level of stress they experienced was revealed by the fact that thirty-four per cent saw the disturbing behaviour of their children as a major problem, thirty-two per cent suffered from loneliness and sexual frustration, twenty-three per cent were worried about what would happen when their husbands were released, and nine per cent suffered from some form of hostility from neighbours or sense of stigma because of their husband's imprisonment.

Although it is stated policy in the British prison system to keep prisoners as close as possible to their families, visiting posed problems for many of the women, whose ability to visit their husbands regularly was limited by distance, expense and the difficulty of travelling with young children. This situation has since improved slightly for such prisoners, but not, of course, for the families of Irish prisoners serving sentences in Britain.

Pauline Morris expressed concern that the stress suffered by the family increased the likelihood of other members, especially the children, becoming social casualties. This concern is the starting point of *Children of Imprisoned Fathers*, by Roger Shaw, published in 1987. He points out that very little work was done on the subject since Pauline Morris's, and asks why.

Answering his own question he postulates: 'As soon as the children of prisoners come into focus the major contradictions of a criminal system become glaringly obvious. When the legally-sanctioned punishment takes the form of incarceration the concept of individual punishment for individual law breaking collapses. Children become caught in the web of punishment.'

Shaw castigates successive British governments for ignoring the plight of children of imprisoned fathers, of whom he estimates there are half a million in England and Wales. They are, he wrote, 'the Cinderella of penology — unrecognised, abused by the system and ignored by those with power and influence'. This is all the more true of prisoners serving long-term sentences for politically-motivated offences, for actions which have aroused the outrage of the entire political, judicial and penal system.

Shaw points out that when a prisoner is sentenced the needs of the family hardly feature in the decision on length of sentence or where it is to be served. All decisions relating to the prisoner stem from the needs of the penal system itself, which are primarily those of containment and security. We may assume that in politically-motivated cases political considerations will also arise. He observes that prisons have an institutionalising effect on inmates and staff alike. This leads to arbitrary interpretation of prison rules, a frequent source of criticism by his respondents. 'Whether or not a woman who states she has lost her Visiting Order gains entry into a prison is said to depend more on her appearance and manner and the attitude of the officer on that gate than on strict interpretation of the regulations. To the officer on duty a woman and her child turned away may be one minor chore in a long day's work but to the woman, who may have travelled a great distance, and particularly to the child, seeing father for the first time for three or four weeks, it is an event creating anger and depression with consequent strife between mother and child.' To a family which has travelled from Ireland for one of the two or three visits in a year which can be afforded, it is a catastrophe.

Shaw's research showed that the economic consequences of imprisonment were usually grave. The families suddenly found themselves in the situation of a one-parent family, with all the poverty characteristic of such families. But one-parent families only have to worry about themselves. Prisoners' families have to worry about the prisoner as well, find the money for visits and, in the North, for the parcels which are so much a part of a prisoner's life.

The women in Shaw's study were often lonely and isolated and sometimes harassed by unwelcome attention from other men who assumed they were available because their partner was away. The mothers among them worried to some extent about the effects of the imprisonment on their children.

Shaw recognises that the effect on the child will be influenced by the individual circumstances of the family, by social class and by the availability of support from others. The relative normality of imprisonment for sections of both communities in the North inevitably affects the way in which the child deals with the imprisonment. But even if she or he sees the father as a hero and maintains a close relationship with him, the loss of the company of one parent throughout her or his childhood will leave a permanent scar.

In Shaw's study, 'the vast majority of women who were interviewed, and teachers, health visitors and others who reported, saw imprisonment of a father as detrimental to many children and sometimes giving rise to serious consequences and a failure to thrive, ill health, disturbed behaviour, truancy and lowered school performance, regardless of the social class or economic group of the family.' Perhaps surprisingly, the effects were worse on the girls.

Those who participated in his survey saw families as punished even more than the prisoners. The prisoners were at least provided with their basic needs of food, clothing and shelter and were protected from outside responsibilities and pressures.

He continues: 'The whole basis of justice and punishment collapses when one repeatedly identifies children of prisoners who suffer more as a result of their father's sentence than did the original victim of the offence. The problem of children of imprisoned fathers has been "swept under the carpet" but unlike many problems this one will not go away; rather the reverse, in time. One hundred thousand children a year are not going to disappear; they are growing older every day, growing up subject to multiple disadvantage and pain, soon to be adolescents and then young adults. We should all know what that means, not only to them but also to the community of which they are members.'

Many of these observations were also made by the National Association for the Care and Resettlement of Offenders (NACRO) in *Forgotten Victims — How Prison Affects the Family*, by Jill Matthews (1983). She also recommends the location of prisoners near their families, better home leave facilities, easing of censorship and restrictions on letters, the doubling of visiting hours and unsupervised family visiting areas, the availability of telephones to all prisoners and longer visits for remand prisoners.

Sparse as they are, all these studies relate to the experience of 'ordinary' prisoners in Britain. Despite twenty years of large-scale imprisonment in Northern Ireland, little has been published on the effects of incarceration on the prisoners themselves and their immediate community. However, one recent study is noteworthy 'Long Term Imprisonment in Northern Ireland: Psychological or Political Survival', by Bill Rolston and Mike Tomlinson (in *Working Papers in European Criminology No 7: The Expansion of European Prison Systems*, ed. Bill Rolston and Mike Tomlinson, 1986).

Rolston and Tomlinson see one of the central functions of prisons as the social isolation and individualisation of the prisoner and the suppression of collective consciousness and action in prisons. They too also highlight the fact that prison places an enormous burden on relationships, and that while relationships with parents, siblings and children are usually maintained, those with wives and girlfriends are much more difficult to keep going.

They point out that, because most long-term prisoners in Northern Ireland would not be in prison but for the political situation, relatives have historically featured strongly in prisoners' support groups. 'The question of how prisoners and their families survive imprisonment, therefore, must be answered within the notion of collective survival.'

Rolston and Tomlinson draw on their interviews with long-term prisoners (republican and loyalist) and their families to show how, although their experience has many similarities with that of other prisoners, it has important differences. Various strategies are drawn up to cope with the imprisonment, foremost among them being the maintenance of family relationships. One woman told them: 'He has said to me that as long as he has me and the kids there, he can do his time, but he couldn't do it on his own. That must be the fear of nearly every man who's inside.'

Among the reasons relationships survive, they include 'the high status of the political prisoners, especially in republican communities. When one woman was asked why she had stuck by her husband — doing life for murder — unlike many British long-term prisoners' wives, she said: "Ach, but they're criminals. If he'd stolen something, I'd have died." The suspicion must be that the position on the loyalist side is less clear-cut and that ambivalence towards political prisoners causes specific problems, especially for relatives.'

The fact that a large number of prisoners are held together, convicted for offences arising out of the same political beliefs, strengthens their commitment and their sense of solidarity. This is not just true of the prisoners. 'Relatives outside, especially women, many of whom may have been politically inactive until their partner's imprisonment, become resolute in their opposition to the state. "The thing that keeps me going, to be quite honest, is that I am determined to fight against this."' This in turn helps them: '"I had to look for some way that I could help him, and having found some way that I thought would help him, that in turn helped me survive."'

Thus Rolston and Tomlinson find an experience shared by the political prisoner and her or his partner very different from that of their 'criminal' counterparts. 'The end result of all this can be a prisoner incorporated into a strong and rewarding collective identity inside the prison, with his or her relatives having the same experience outside. The visit, finally, becomes the interface where the two aspects of this solidarity meet,' though they concede: 'There are prisoners who do not make it, who succumb to the individualisation of prison and turn, for example, to drugs.' Equally, there are prisoners' partners who find the burden intolerable and who end the relationship, despite strong community pressure not to do so. But overall, the authors conclude, 'collective solidarity and political ideology is a major element in the survival of prisoners and their relatives in the Northern Ireland case.'

Their study concentrated on prisoners from a republican background. The Reverend William James Hughes, who was the presbyterian chaplain in the Maze Prison (Long Kesh) from 1983 until his sudden death in November 1989, completed that year an MSc dissertation on *The Effect of Life Imprisonment on Families* for the University of Ulster, which concentrated on the experiences of loyalist prisoners.

'The lives of these families have', he wrote, 'been devastated with an ongoing suffering, worse in some ways than bereavement, and for whom in many cases the only solution is to divorce themselves from the prisoner, and sever all links with him.'

Although no figures are available, marriage breakdown seems to be much higher among loyalist than republican prisoners. Hughes finds that with loyalist prisoners the marriage which survives is the exception. Although marriage breakdown is common among republican prisoners, many marriages do survive, at least for the duration of the sentence. According to Tony Caffney of the Sinn Féin department dealing with prisoners and their families, the breakdown often comes after release.

Hughes makes a distinction between loyalist prisoners who came into prison ten and more years ago, who felt they had to do what they did because their areas were under attack and they no longer felt the police and army could adequately defend them, and those who have come in more recently, whom he describes as 'the children of violence'. Most of the former now regret what they did and accept that they deserve punishment for taking life. The latter, however, 'assume a tough "macho" image — truculent, aggressive, cynical and at time, exceedingly hostile . . . there does seem to be a greater criminal element involved nowadays'.

There is differentiation among the relatives also. 'Life sentences usually produce both dismemberment and demoralisation, but if a man's wife, for example, is passionately committed to the same cause, supports him in his activities and sees him as a hero, her experience of facing his life sentence will not be the same as that of other women. If she comes from an area which supports paramilitarism, and in which she and he are approved and admired, that too will influence her experience. There will be no stigma attached to crime or family. Indeed the kudos attracted by the sentence may to some small degree compensate for the separation. . . On the other hand, as one would expect, it was found that other women were resentful, and blamed the prisoner for getting them into an impossible situation. They were hurt and bewildered, humiliated and deeply distressed.'

In many cases the imprisonment of their husbands came as a great shock to the women who did not know of their involvement. Unlike the republican prisoners, many of the loyalists had well-paid jobs before their imprisonment and the families were accustomed to a fairly high standard of living. This was drastically reduced by the imprisonment, though the worst effects were usually ameliorated by the support of their extended family. Nonetheless, the woman had to face a reduction in her circumstances while at the same time learning to cope both as a single parent family and with all the prison regulations.

Whether the marriage survived or ended in divorce, the woman had to play a very different role in the family and in society as a whole, and this brought about changes in her and in the relationship. Often this brought tension later, sometimes after the prisoner's release, when he found it difficult to adjust to her new role, and she could not accept his attempt to assume the position he had in the family before his imprisonment.

Like Shaw, Hughes found that the children bore their own burden, with many of them becoming withdrawn, difficult and troublesome. Yet 'some mothers do contrive to contain the damage to their children. . . Some prisoners' families have been very successful, with children distinguishing themselves in academic, cultural and sporting fields, and the key has often been an able and gifted mother.' However, he sees the trauma of the children who do suffer as worse than bereavement. 'Bereavement will pass for such children, but the life-sentenced prisoner's children never comes to that state. The father is not there, but neither is he completely absent, so the hurt of the child never heals.'

Hughes concludes with a list of recommendations to improve the lot of the prisoners and their families, including much more planned preparation for their eventual release, involving the family. Hughes argues that prisoners' wives and children, who are victims of a tragedy they did not create, are of the utmost value. 'They require and deserve the compassion of the society of which they are, and will remain, an integral part. So let them not be pushed out into communities of their own.'

Not Just Victims

All these studies, with the exception of Rolston and Tomlinson's, see the families primarily as victims. But there is another dimension to their collective experience. The imprisonment for different periods of some 10,000 people, the overwhelming majority of them men, has transformed relationships within their families. Those left with responsibility for running the family have usually been women who have had to take on providing for the economic as well as the emotional well-being of the family and the up-bringing of the children while also trying to give material, emotional and moral support to the prisoner. Given the nature of his offence, they have also frequently found themselves in conflict with the authorities, with whom they must negotiate visits, letters and general access to the prisoner. In cases of wrongful conviction, it has been the families of the prisoners who have pursued their cases, learning about the law, exploring the legal and penal system, lobbying politicians, churchmen, journalists and other public figures.

Of course, there have been, and are still, women prisoners convicted for politically-motivated offences. In March 1990 there were twenty-one female prisoners in Maghaberry prison, of whom seventeen were linked with the IRA (there were no loyalist female prisoners). There are two Irish women in the high security H-Wing of Durham prison in Britain. This does not include Judith Ward, the young English woman convicted of the M62 bombing, whose friends maintain she was wrongfully convicted. Further afield, Pauline Drumm is awaiting trial in France for alleged IRA offences committed on the continent.

The experience of these women, all of them very young when arrested, is unique in Europe and is not without interest. However, from the point of view of the community as a whole the impact of their imprisonment on their families is similar to that of their male counterparts. Again, it is frequently the female members of their families, mothers and sisters, who bear the brunt of keeping in touch and of looking after their dependants.

This has led to a changed perspective of women's role in the community. Hester Dunne of Justice for Lifers, an action group for life-sentenced loyalist prisoners, said: 'I know men don't have it in them to do what women have done. This is not a criticism of particular individuals; it's just men in general.'

Tony Caffney of Sinn Féin described the changes as follows: 'The wives are forced to take on all sorts of responsibilities they didn't have before. They get to see a sort of life they want to keep up. Relatives involved in campaign work would have said they were happy before with their home life. Now they're even sitting down to do interviews, which they would have refused to do when their husbands were there.' Hugh, a republican ex-prisoner who served seventeen years, added: 'When the men get out there's a very deep sense of pride in their families and wives.'

There may be pride, and there is certainly strong community support for prisoners' families in republican areas (it is more patchy in loyalist areas), but this can be claustrophobic. A lot is expected of relatives, and it is not always possible to match these expectations. Those who fall beneath the expectations of the community and extended family in terms of fidelity and support for their partner pay a price in increased isolation and withdrawal of community solidarity.

If this happens, the mantle of 'first relative' falls to a mother, sister, daughter or, more rarely, a male relative. Of course, where a prisoner is unmarried, his blood relatives already play the major supporting role. Taking on this responsibility alters the economy and lifestyle of the whole family. Holidays take second place to the weekly visit (if the prisoner is in Northern Ireland), and provision must be made for the regular parcels (which cost about £30 to make up). Where a family is surviving on low wages or social welfare — and the majority of prisoners come from areas of high unemployment — this imposes a considerable extra burden.

The weight of the problems is multiplied many times when the prisoner is in Britain. The sentences are usually very long (there are people still in prison in Britain who were jailed in 1973), and review and remission practices are much less generous than in Northern Ireland. Visits are less frequent, so it is more difficult to keep the relationship going.

Visits also cost much more. Instead of being able to take the bus (usually subsidised by the organisation to which the prisoner belongs), the relative must embark on a journey which involves trains, boats or planes, more trains, buses or taxis, to a high security prison buried somewhere in the English countryside. Bed and breakfast accommodation must be found and meals in restaurants paid for. If there are children they must be transported, fed, accommodated and, if they are young, amused. While people in the North in receipt of Social Welfare get a subsidy towards the cost of prison visits to close relatives, this is never enough. Sarah Conlon, who worked as an orderly in the Royal Victoria Hospital for very low wages, never got a penny. There is no assistance for people living in the Republic who need to visit relatives in Britain.

All these problems have given rise to a wide range of organisations supporting the demand of the prisoners and their relatives that they be transferred to Northern Ireland, so far to no avail.

The Wrongly Convicted

While the families of prisoners have to deal with the problems of separation, poverty and stress, the burden is even greater when they are convinced of the innocence of the prisoner, as was the

29

case with the Birmingham Six, the Guildford Four and other, less notorious, cases. The suffering is combined with bewilderment, anger and a great sense of loss which even their release will not relieve. In the words of Sarah Conlon, 'they just seemed to take part of my life away. Most people think now with Gerry being out it's all right, but you won't forget the hard years that you've been through.'

If, as is usually the case, the prisoners were not members of the armed organisations responsible for the crime they are held to have committed, their families will neither seek nor receive the solidarity and support of the relatives' networks linked to these organisations. Where the offences have been committed in Britain and the men convicted and sentenced there, they must face the hostility engendered by the crime with no support network to turn to. Despised by republican supporters for repudiating the republican campaign, they encounter the enmity of those who oppose it.

They have the additional burden of trying to prove the innocence of the prisoner. The mothers, sisters, daughters, wives (and some uncles, brothers-in-law and sons as well) of the Birmingham Six and the Guildford Four report the long, weary years of trudging from door to door, from public figure to public figure, to explain why the individuals concerned could not have committed the crimes of which they were accused, only to be met with disbelief in most quarters.

When gradually that changed and different elements in the media began to be interested, new pressures came. The women became public figures themselves as they gave interviews, spoke at public meetings, engaged in debate with lawyers and politicians. Gratitude for the support of the media has become tinged with cynicism as, in the case of the Birmingham Six, the men were still in jail at the end of 1990. As Breda Power, the daughter of Billy Power said: 'I've been talking about my feelings for years and where has it got us? They're all still inside. We've turned ourselves inside out for the media. When we want them to do something for us it's a different story.'

Yet the years of prison visiting, of fighting the authorities, of campaigning for the release of the men, have changed these women. For the younger ones campaigning is now part of life, and they have said that when the men are out they will continue to campaign for other victims of miscarriages of justice. Sandra Hunter, the English wife of Gerry Hunter, one of the Birmingham Six, now has a very changed attitude to the police and judicial system she was brought up to respect.

This new-found independence and self-reliance begs the question — at what cost? This is not the first time women have been thrust into the foreground by personal catastrophe or community suffering, and have surprised observers by their capabilities. The wives of the British miners during the 1984 strike and the sisters of Brian Keenan are recent examples. But must it take catastrophe for women to enter the public arena? They may have grown as a result of suffering, but the suffering usually resulted, not from their own freely-decided-upon actions, but those of their menfolk. What happens when the strike is over, when their brother is released, when their husbands, sons and fathers come out of jail? So far, the depressing lesson is that, with few exceptions, they fade back into the background, that there is little of permanence to show for all that sacrifice, all that work. As it is, they have no organised voice. This is partly a reflection of the position of the communities from which the prisoners come, who either have no political figures speaking for them (in the case of the loyalists) or have their political representatives ostracised by other politicians and the media (in the case of the republicans). It is also a reflection of the general difficulty of those on the underbelly of society, women, children, the poor (and these are usually women) in having their voices heard.

Yet surely this is no reason for the 100,000 or so people affected one way or another by imprisonment in the North of Ireland to be so comprehensively ignored? How can the problems of the North be addressed without considering the views and feelings of those who have suffered most from them?

Chapter One

Dealing with
Imprisonment in Britain

One of the features of the most recent IRA campaign has been attacks on targets in Britain itself. Since the early 1970s there have been sporadic bombings of pubs and sites associated with the British army or with politicians and members of the judiciary, and also of civilian sites such as Harrods and the London Underground. These bombings have resulted in a number of deaths and serious injuries.

Predictably, this has led to in outrage in Britain and pressure on the police to catch and punish the perpetrators. In the early 1970s this task was carried out with more enthusiasm than discrimination, and led to a number of wrongful convictions of Irish people living and working in Britain, the most notorious of which were the cases of the Birmingham Six, the Guildford Four and the Maguire Seven. Others arrested and convicted in this period were the Price sisters, along with four male colleagues, the Gillespie sisters, the Balcombe Street group, Frank Stagg and the English woman, Judith Ward.

The Price sisters, Dolours and Marion, along with two of their co-convicted, Hugh Feeny and Gerry Kelly, went on hunger strike demanding transfer back to Northern Ireland in order to serve their sentences closer to their families. Effectively they won their case. The then Home Secretary, Roy Jenkins, said he saw no reason why they should not serve the bulk of their lengthy sentences nearer their families. Some months after the end of the hunger strike they were transferred back to Northern Ireland. The Price sisters, who were suffering from anorexia, were released on health grounds after serving seven and a half and eight years of their sentences.

They were to be the last transferees. One of their co-defendants is still in prison in Britain. (Another was transferred and eventually released after serving seventeen years, but the prison department later said this had been a mistake.) According to Gareth Peirce, a lawyer who has represented dozens of Irish defendants, 'over one hundred republican prisoners have since sweated it out in England.'

In 1977 Frank Stagg, originally from County Mayo, went on hunger strike following the rejection of his request for a transfer. The British government was adamant that there was no basis to his request, as his wife, and therefore his primary family connection, was from Coventry. He died on hunger strike, and his funeral in Ireland was one of the more farcical episodes in the history of the coalition government in Dublin, when his coffin was seized by Gardaí and buried under several feet of concrete. It was later dug up by the IRA and given a republican funeral.

Since then almost all requests from Irish prisoners serving sentences in Britain for politically-motivated crimes have been refused. Shane Paul O'Doherty from Derry, who was convicted of sending letter bombs, was an exception. He was transferred to prison in Northern Ireland, but only after he publicly repudiated the IRA and his previous political convictions. It is widely perceived that this is a condition for a successful transfer application.

However, this is not the stated policy of the Home Office or of the prison service. According to the prison rules: 'consideration shall be given to a prisoner and his family to maintain long-term contact . . . all prisoners are entitled to one statutory visit a month and one discretionary visit.' The specific regulation covering the transfer of a prisoner comes from Section 26 (1) of the 1961 Criminal Justice Act: 'The responsible minister may, on the application of a person serving a sentence of imprisonment or detention in any part of the United Kingdom, make an order for his transfer to another part of the United Kingdom . . . there to serve the remainder of his sentence, and for his removal to an appropriate institution there.' The law further requires that the minister decide on the basis of 'relevant considerations'.

The wording of this makes it clear that the prisoner has no right to transfer. The minister has total discretion in the matter, and the 'relevant considerations' which have been cited to refuse transfers leave the suspicion that serving the full sentence in Britain is seen as part of the punishment for the crime.

When an Irish prisoner serves a sentence in Britain the punishment inflicted on the family is much greater than that suffered by him (or her). The conditions in the high security units where Irish prisoners serve their sentences are harsher than those operating in prisons like Long Kesh in Northern Ireland. These prisoners also lack the companionship and solidarity of hundreds of political colleagues. But there is usually more than one Irish prisoner in each high security unit, and they have access to education and recreational facilities, though this varies with the prison. Above all, they are sure of their food and shelter, and, while many Irish prisoners have been mistreated by prison warders, especially in the mid-1970s, their families also report instances of compassion and humanity.

For the family, the arrest, conviction and sentencing of a relative in Britain is a catastrophe. They must find the resources, financial, emotional and mental, for years, maybe decades, of travel to Britain to maintain contact with their loved one. Often they are nervous on these journeys, fearful that they might be arrested under the Prevention of Terrorism Act (PTA). Mothers with young children are afraid that this might result in their children being taken into care if both parents end up in custody. Another fear is of exclusion from Britain under the PTA, for which no reason need be given. If someone is excluded from Britain it means she or he will never be able to visit their relative in prison there again.

For parents the worry is that they will grow too old and frail to make the journey, and face an old age with the knowledge that they will never see their daughter or son again. For them a long sentence in Britain for a daughter or son almost amounts to a death sentence. Some suffer from heart complaints or high blood pressure and the journey puts further strain on their health. A number of Irish prisoners have seen their parents die while they are in prison. Parole to see a dying parent, or to attend a relative's funeral, is not given to these prisoners.

This is just one of the many differences between the experience of prisoners in Britain and that of people who commit similar offences in Northern Ireland or, indeed, in the Republic. Other differences arise long before they are imprisoned.

The first discrepancy arises when they are charged. If a person is found in possession of explosives, a weapon or a list of the names and addresses of police or public figures in Northern Ireland, he or she will face different charges than they would in the same circumstances in Britain. In the North, the charges will relate to the precise offence — possession of guns or explosives or of information likely to be of use to terrorists. These carry sentences ranging from eighteen months to eight years (life, if intent to murder is proven). In Britain, however, they are likely to be charged with conspiracy to cause explosions or to murder. Conspiracy charges relate to offences not necessarily committed at all, but to the intention to commit a crime. Yet they carry sentences equal to, and sometimes greater than, those for the crime itself. For example, two young men convicted in December 1990 of conspiracy to cause explosions (not with causing any specific explosion) were sentenced to thirty years imprisonment. A murder conviction carries a life sentence which in practice amounts to less than twenty years, unless a minimum sentence is specified. Some life sentenced prisoners are released in less than ten years.

As Gareth Peirce put it: 'You have people in jail in England from Northern Ireland who were either not involved or were involved marginally, or who did something, but the prosecution never got the evidence against them. The evidence is often not there to support the substantive charge so a conspiracy charge is brought in to cover it instead. So here "possession" becomes conspiracy to cause explosions in England. Then the sentences are much longer. For example, one of my clients here would have got eight years in Northern Ireland and been released after four. But because he was arrested and tried in England he got sixteen years, which the judge described as "lenient" because he was elderly, and he will serve ten and a half.'

People with republican views adopt a philosophical attitude

to being convicted for an offence. Even if the evidence against them is less than would secure a conviction for the substantive offence, they usually don't fight the case very hard. Most activists feel that, if you become involved at all, you take your chances and face the possibility of a prison sentence or even death. One woman, when asked if she had expected her husband to be arrested, replied: 'I didn't expect him to be arrested in connection with England.'

Tony Caffney of Sinn Féin's prisoners' department, who himself served fifteen years as an SOSP prisoner (on the Secretary of State's Pleasure) outlined the organisation's policy: 'We say no Irish person receives a fair trial before a British court. Now that's tinged with a fair degree of pragmatism, because if we say someone is innocent we imply that someone else is guilty. Then you have to be careful. People use different things to keep them going, they often have illusions, and it may not be right to take them from them.' This seems to imply that it may be better for the family to think their relative is guilty than to have to endure years of fruitless and exhausting battle against conviction, like the families of the Birmingham Six. As Gareth Peirce put it, 'There's not enough emotional energy to deal with everything.' Obviously, finding it easier to accept the possibility that the relative did commit the offence only applies to those from a community which generally supports the IRA.

Once imprisoned, further discrepancies arise. Until last year prisoners in Northern Ireland could hope for a fifty per cent remission of their sentences, while in England only one third remission prevails. This difference in penal practice has been the main reason given by the Home Office recently in refusing to allow prisoners in Britain to transfer to Northern Ireland. Since the most recent renewal of the Prevention of Terrorism Act, however, one third remission has been brought in in Northern Ireland, so the distinction no longer applies.

Prisoners in Northern Ireland, and in the Republic, normally serve all their sentences in the same prison. In England they are frequently moved from one high security unit to another (except for women high security prisoners, as Durham has the only unit for them in Britain). One prisoner arrested in 1973 has been moved seventy times. It sometimes happens that the family arrives from Ireland to visit the prisoner only to be told that he has just been moved. The family must then spend more money, and precious time, travelling to the other prison.

There are a few groups and individuals who help the families of Irish prisoners in Britain. Foremost among them is Sister Sarah Clarke, a nun who has been visiting remand prisoners, meeting their families when they come to visit, putting them up when necessary, accompanying them to the court hearings and generally offering friendship and support. Again and again when I was talking to relatives of Irish prisoners in Britain, they said: 'I don't know what I'd have done without Sister Sarah.' But she and her colleagues can only provide fire-brigade action against the sense of vulnerability and isolation families feel when visiting prisons in Britain.

All of these problems compound the difficulties of a prisoner maintaining her or his relationships with her or his family. Because of the distance, time and expense, visits can take place only two or three times a year, when the total visiting entitlements are accumulated and the visitor can have two visits a day over three or four days. In between, the prisoner and his or her family must rely on letters. What is remarkable is the number of relationships which survive in these circumstances.

Mary

Mary has been visiting her husband Roy in prison in England for seventeen years. She was twenty-three when he was arrested with the Price sisters. He was twenty-four, and they had been married three years. Their son Patrick was one year and four months old, and Mary was pregnant with their daughter Róisín, born two weeks after his arrest.

Roy was arrested on 8 March and sentenced on 11 November 1974 in Winchester court. He was sentenced to two life sentences and twenty years for bombing offences. Mary settled down to the years of visiting.

In the early days the visiting conditions were very harsh. She faced the constant fear that he would not be in the prison when she got there, or that he would be protesting about the visiting conditions and would suffer as a result, or that she would lose the visit. 'Once I went there and he should have been on the Isle of Wight. I had to take two boats, a train and bus. Then I found he had been moved. They said they knew they would move him only twenty four hours before. I had to go up to Leeds with the bags and everything. Patrick would have been about four and Róisín two and a half. She was in a buggy and was still in nappies. When we got to Amley in Leeds it was only a remand prison and we could only have a half-hour visit. He's been moved about seventy times altogether.

'One time I went to Gartree. There had been a bit of a row over visiting conditions, and they stopped a visit that morning. We protested, and they called the police. When the police came and saw it was only us and the kids they couldn't believe it! We were only off the boat that morning, but they wouldn't give us back our visits. Roy was moved again that day.

'The closed visits were frustrating. You couldn't really talk. All you could talk about was the travelling and the journey; there was no time really to talk about anything else. We used to have to talk through a grille, and you couldn't hear. One time Roy went on the roof to protest about the visiting conditions. He had no visits for six or seven months.

'Wakefield was the worst place he was in. He was in a padded cell. He was protesting about the conditions. All he did was protest about the conditions and what happened to him. It used to worry me what it was doing to him, being moved all the time. He was in solitary confinement a lot of the time.

'Roy's mother was very, very ill after he was arrested. She could not travel; she was in a wheelchair after four heart attacks. She didn't see him for seven years, and then she died. He took it awful, awful bad. It nearly killed him. God was on our side that I was over at the time. I didn't know what to say and he's my husband. He hadn't seen her for seven years. After the funeral his sisters and brothers went over to see him. My mother loved him, but she couldn't bear to go over and see him and then leave him behind.

'He's in Gartree now; he has been there for two and a half

years. It's the longest spell he's spent anywhere. This last couple of years it's not too bad. The visiting conditions are an awful lot better.'

Despite this, Mary and Roy have managed to communicate and to keep their relationship going. The children are devoted to their father, who is kept in touch with everything they do. They are now old enough to visit alone, and do so, sometimes bringing their girl- or boy-friends with them.

'The first day of the visit he's usually uptight,' continued Mary, 'He relaxes then as the visits go on, and gets tense again towards the end. If he was over here we'd be up to see him every week. Why they never transferred him is beyond me. He's still there and the rest of those arrested with him are out now.

'He hated his letters being censored. He used to say his problems were his and his family's alone. Sometimes I still get a letter, "are you alright, are the kids alright?" and that would be it, nothing personal in them at all. We only exchange personal things on a visit.

'If the screws searched the kids or touched them in any way it would do his head in. When Patrick started school, he was only four, he was delighted with his new school-bag and he wanted to show it to his Daddy. The screw wouldn't let him; he wouldn't allow any physical contact at all. Roy went wild. That was in Wakefield. It was terrible.'

Mary has another daughter, born when Roy had been in prison for twelve years. 'For seven months I never told anybody I was pregnant. I told the kids first. They were raging with me that I didn't tell them, that I kept it bottled up inside. I went over then and told him. Sister Sarah came with me to the prison, and waited outside while I went in to see him. I didn't know how he'd take it.

'I told him, and the two of us cried and we sorted it out. I brought her (the baby) over to see him then when she was a few weeks old, so the bond's there between the two of them. She idolises him now, and he her. She sits on his shoulders the whole visit. He loves her even more than his own. He'll be with her growing up, so he won't have missed out on all that, like he did with the other two.

39

'One visit Roy was paying me a lot of attention, and she was playing with a screw and not getting much attention. She said something to him (the screw), and when I heard her I almost died, but he just looked up and winked. The older ones are grand. You get the younger ones coming in and they all want stripes and they say you do this and you do that. There's no way Roy will stand for that; he's been there so long. But this one said, "You shouldn't punish the child as well. Especially with you coming so far".'

Mary has the support of the local community and her family, and this helped her survive the seventeen years of her husband's imprisonment. 'The neighbours could not be better that time when I was pregnant. Anyway, why should you worry about what people are saying? If you did you'd never get on with your own life. They can say what they like about these flats, but it's a good community.

'My mummy is only dead six years. She was a great strength, and so were my brothers. It's a great help when you have a good family. I was never in touch with NIACRO (*the Northern Ireland Association for the Care and Resettlement of Offenders*) or any of those people. Years ago I used to go to meetings and be on all sorts of committees, but nothing came out of them and you get disheartened. I think sometimes when you're a bit independent, maybe you can be too independent, but you manage. When you have your family it means a lot.'

When she spoke to me she was very optimistic that Roy would soon be released, and was eagerly awaiting the outcome of a judicial review of his case. 'All he talks about is coming out. He wants to go away for a while. Then he wants to build his own house and spend all the time he can with his family.'

A few days after the interview she learned that a decision on his release date had been deferred for five years. However, in March he was granted leave to appeal against the sentence.

Geraldine

Geraldine's experience of the British criminal justice system began ten years after Mary's, and she missed some of the worst years, in the mid 1970s. But her life cannot be regarded as easy.

Tragedy hit her early when her first husband, Seán, was killed in an explosion. She was nineteen, he was twenty. They had been married for three years, and had one daughter, Seáneen. This experience has coloured her attitude to the imprisonment of her second husband, Tommy, in 1983, for murder and causing an explosion. 'At least he's alive and sitting there, and he'll be home some day. Seán will never come home.'

Tommy was a close friend of Seán's, and helped Geraldine when he died. They became closer, and after a time they started to live together and had a daughter, Danielle, now ten. Seáneen has a clear memory of Tommy living with them and acting as her father until she was seven. Danielle was only two when he was arrested, and only knows him through prison visits and letters.

Geraldine is an attractive woman who laughs easily and often describes her experiences with humour. She has managed to maintain a very close relationship with Tommy through letters and visits. 'I'm not much good for writing. I've my letter every week — it used to be two a week, but he's put me on punishment for not writing! If we ever split up it'll be over me not writing. To me the visits are the most important.

'I go over between four and six times a year on accumulated visits. I get one hour in the morning and two hours in the afternoon. The kids come over about twice a year. Then the morning visit is mine and the afternoon one is theirs. I don't get a word in then! Now that Seáneen is seventeen she can go on her own and take Danielle in. For seven years Tommy has never sat with the kids without me. Next Easter he'll get a visit with Seáneen alone and one with her and Danielle.'

The visits have not been without problems. 'When he was lifted here and taken over to England I went on a visit and I was lifted and held for forty eight hours. I was strip-searched. I didn't have the kids with me, thank God. My whole fear was that I would be lifted and they would be taken into care. I've said to the kids, "If they lift me, hold on to me and don't let go." That way they'd have had to put the kids into the cell with me. Another time he was in Full Sutton and for some reason I hadn't booked a B and B. The one I went to said they were full, and I was just walking around the roads with the kids and Danielle said "It's all right for me Daddy. He's got a roof over his head."

'The time of the hurricane we arrived in our summer clothes, soaked, and the screw said, "You're not getting in." He was one of the nastiest screws I ever met. My nerves were gone. I had a big suitcase on wheels with me and I just threw it in and threw the kids in after it.' She laughed as she demonstrated. 'I said, "I'm getting in even for five minutes." Then another screw came and asked, "Did you get caught in the hurricane?" and the first one said, "When I left Sandy Row this morning it wasn't raining," to show me where he came from. I got in.

'It's worth it all when you get in. On the visit I don't talk about politics, I don't talk about back home, I don't talk about the troubles. It's about me and him and the kids. He's always in good form, even times I'm not. There's times I'd go over wanting to fight and he won't let me.'

Preparing for the visit is an elaborate business. 'I get all my best clothes, and I borrow jewellery from my friends. The kids are all dressed up as well. I get up at half past seven to do my hair (Geraldine is a hairdresser), and put on my make-up. He wouldn't know me if he saw me at home!'

They were married three years ago in Albany prison on the Isle of Wight. It was their fourth attempt to formalise their relationship since Tommy went to prison. 'The security was terrible. You would have thought I'd have put him in my pocket and walked home with him. The whole place was cordoned off while we were in the prison. There were choppers and dogs everywhere and men on the roofs. Then they told me it would be a registry office wedding and demanded another £30.

'They'd promised sandwiches and said that we could take photographs with our own cameras. There were no sandwiches made and our cameras were not allowed. A screw took photos. There were screws all around the walls while we were taking our vows.

'There was a priest there who gave a blessing, and Tommy's mummy wanted a photo of him. They refused, and there was an argument, and his mummy fainted. He rushed over to her and started to cry, and I rushed over to him crying to see if he was all right. After all that a screw came over offering him a knife and asking him, "Do you want to cut the cake?" It sounds funny now, but it wasn't funny then. Apart from the day that Seán died, that was the worst day of my life.'

Upstairs she produced the album of wedding photographs, showing a dark, slight man dressed in a new suit, her in a wedding dress, the two girls and four other members of the family. Her room is full of the pictures Tommy has painted in the prison, carefully-executed portraits of the family, idealised country scenes and detailed narrative paintings. Like many Irish prisoners in Britain and politically-motivated prisoners in the North, he is completing an Open University course, studying social science and politics.

The conditions in each prison are different. 'In Full Sutton, where he is now, there's a wee bit more privacy. The screws sit in an adjoining room or the corridor. Sometimes they put a newspaper in front of their face, or fall asleep, to give you more privacy. That's the first jail I've been to where that happens.'

As she speaks, the strength of the relationship between the couple is striking. She recounts the discussions they have through the letters and during the visits in great detail. 'I tell him everything. I tell him if I look sideways. There's no point in having a relationship if you don't share the downs as well as the ups.

'He's definitely an atheist. He accuses me of brain-washing the kids in the catholic religion, and I accuse him of not giving them anything. I say they need something. They need not practise if they like when they grow up. If they don't want to go to mass I don't force them. But they go if they want to.

'He didn't want her doing her First Communion. I never did bring her over in the dress. Then when he got the photo of her in it he said, "Who'd have thought that when our Danielle was born she'd marry the most famous man in the world?" My mummy is very religious and sometimes she blesses herself when we talk about him.

'He wanted me to send Danielle to Lisburn to the integrated school and all that. Here's me: "There's a school at the bottom of the road." When he gets out he can take them down to Lisburn.'

43

She talks openly about the problem of enforced celibacy and her own fidelity. 'He says to me I should have the odd — you know (*looking at the children*) — and never tell him. He doesn't know how I've lasted. He says if it ever happens it'll never split us. But it's not in my nature. If I did I'd be splitting.

'I haven't promised Tommy I'll wait on him. I've said, I'll try. I've said "I'll be with you until I can't take it any more." I go out and go to parties and that, and I sit in men's company and leave with men, but that's all. I know women with men inside and they're afraid to talk to a man in case their fella would crack. I don't want a situation where I can't tell him who's in and out of the house. He did comment on one man who visited here that he didn't like him. There was a bit of jealousy there. I was chuffed!

'Say I started seeing someone, casually at first. Then if it got serious, think of the person you were in love with, you had children with and who's your friend, and the pain you'd cause him. I say to Tommy when he talks like that, "Catch yourself on. It's enough for me to bring up the two girls."

'I lie and read his letters three or four times. If I say something wrong, he's consoling me. He says over and over how much he loves me. It's brilliant, like. There's times our letters cross and we're saying the same thing. I don't look at Tommy as just my husband. He's my friend, my closest friend. The fact that I had a good relationship is standing to me now.'

One of the most difficult things is bringing up children alone. 'You miss him when the kids are annoying you. I'm the authority figure with the kids. They have this Daddy who never shouts at them but tells me to leave them alone. He only gets twenty hours with his kids in the whole year and he can't be expected to shout at them. Sometimes you feel you're carrying the whole three of them. Seáneen is a teenager now and what she put me through last year was mustard. Say she wants to go out when she should be studying, and Danielle wants to go out. By the time they're sorted out I'm up to ninety and I say, "I'm sick of all three of yez." They only get twenty hours a year with their Daddy and they did nothing.

'I get great support from the committee (*of relatives of prisoners in England*). It's like a support group. If he's moved to a jail he's not been in before they'll tell you all about the bus routes and the B and Bs and all that. But that only took off in the past few years.'

Despite her involvement with the committee for the transfer of prisoners, she does not regard herself as a political person. 'I was never politically involved in anything; it's just my kids and my husband. I'm just involved in the committee because my husband's in jail. I had Seáneen when I was sixteen and I'd never do anything that would take me away from her. I'm not IRA and I'm not SDLP either. I look at things as they arise.'

Like other prisoners' wives, she had to take on additional responsibilities when Tommy went to prison. 'I relied on him an awful lot. I never even wrote a note for the school when he was here, though I ran the money. Now when you make a decision you just hope it's the right one.'

She is coping. A few months ago she sold the small house they had owned and bought a larger one in a new development on the edge of West Belfast, raising a mortgage to add to the price of the old house. 'I told him I'd be cutting back on the visits, but he'll be coming home to it.'

However, her experiences have affected her attitude to authority. Seáneen can visit her father alone now that she is sixteen, and she had to be passed by the police because he is a Category A (high security) prisoner. 'She had to go in to Grosvenor Road police station. We were brought up to the top of the building and verbally abused. She was asked about her pals, and accused of shop-lifting and glue-sniffing. They accused me of having men in and out of the house, and when I asked who, they named my two brothers!

'The more I thought about it as the days went by the more angry I got. I contacted a solicitor and the complaint has gone through three stages now. What I want to show Seáneen is that she has her rights and she does not have to suffer because of her father's politics. He has his politics and I have my political views and she has hers.'

Tommy has several times applied for transfer to a prison in Northern Ireland, but he has always been refused. 'The NIO (*Northern Ireland Office*) blames the Home Office and the Home

Office blames the NIO. David Wall of NIACRO says that it's the Home Office, not the NIO, that is objecting to transfers because of the parole here. The Home Office wants them to serve at least twenty years.' However, the discrepancy on remission has now been removed.

Unless Tommy gets a transfer Geraldine must face another thirteen years of saving for visits three or four times a year at most, otherwise relying on letters to maintain contact with her husband. If he was in prison in Northern Ireland she could at least hope for a few days' home leave in the summer and at Christmas when he had served twelve years. If he serves the twenty years, she will be forty seven when he is released. The time they will have spent together can be counted in hours.

Chrissie

Chrissie is into the home stretch. Her husband Brian was convicted of conspiracy to cause explosions in 1978 and is due for release this year (1991).

He is serving an additional three years because of an attempted escape shortly after his arrest. Chrissie was arrested in December of that year, suspected of complicity with the escape attempt. 'I was held in Brixton on remand for six months. I had six children between the ages of eleven and about seventeen. Anne-Marie, the eldest, got pregnant while I was in Brixton. It really knocked me for six that it had happened and I wasn't even here.

'We were in Brixton together at the time. I had a feeling that something was wrong. I wrote to her saying if she had any problem she should tell me. Then a social worker called me in and said, "I have a bit of bad news for you." I said, "Is it Anne-Marie?" and she said, "You know." I said, "No", and she said, "She's pregnant." I just went to pieces then worrying about her.

'Then I was able to write to my friend here and get her to keep an eye on her. I kept thinking what state of mind she must have been in. The kids coped, though. My family was very good, but I'm still hearing stories about what happened "when you weren't here".

'I applied for bail so many times, and they kept turning me down. The police said I would abscond. Even the judge laughed at that — with six children — but he could do nothing. It was used as additional pressure on Brian. It was nearly fifteen months before the trial came up, and at one stage he was told his wife could walk out the gate if he signed papers. I was very angry. I saw I was being used, and it made me more determined to go on.

'Eventually I got out on bail on condition that I stayed in Britain. I stayed with relatives of Brian and I was there for his trial. The kids were able to come over on visits and that, but they could not stay. Anne-Marie had the baby.

'During his trial I didn't understand it at all, it was all new to me. I had never been in a court in my life. I had never even been in a police station. I didn't even understand my own trial. I was acquitted; there was no evidence against me whatsoever.

'Then I came home and I started visiting from here. I knew I was watched all the time. I got over three or four times a year depending on the weather. I wasn't working, just living on the single parents' allowance. You're just saving, saving, saving. The social welfare is a help towards the visits, but you need a lot more.'

Like many of those whose only experience of England is visiting someone in prison there, she found it all very intimidating. 'It's frightening, going to a foreign country. Sometimes they won't accept Northern Ireland money. That was one of the main problems. I used to get all uptight about it in the shops. I decided it wasn't worth it, I was so stressed up going on a visit anyway. I used to change the money in the bank before I went.

'You were more worried about the kids going over as they grew up. I used to sit here watching the clock, timing them, thinking where they were at each stage. It was a long time before I'd let them go on their own. They were pulled in and questioned a few times.'

Chrissie has her own strategy for keeping the relationship with her husband going. 'You don't think about it very much. If you did you would just get depressed. Most women feel the same. You marry them for better or worse, and you have to take the bad with the good. I would never think of not going to see him. It's a lonely life, but what can you do?

'I had money problems and that, but I didn't talk about them. He couldn't do anything about it. He has to know about problems at home with the family, though. He never tells me about his problems. He tells me he has none, but I know he has.

'Neither of us was from a republican family. His was the opposite — his father was in the air force for twenty three years. He was never interned, he had never been arrested before. When he was arrested here and taken to Castlereagh I was shocked. I asked him why and he said he didn't know. The last time we'd been in England was when we were married. That was thirty years ago. I'm not a political person at all. I never ever was. I'm not interested in politics. I don't understand them for a start. The kids have never had any hassle or anything. None of them got involved, thank God. I don't know if I could have handled it if they did. I always counted myself lucky in that respect.'

Brian sought to keep very close links with his family. 'That was his main worry. They're very, very close to him. They write and tell him things they wouldn't tell me. When the children got married he always wrote out a speech to be read out at the wedding. We always had videos of the weddings made for him. Four of the six are married now, and there are nine grandchildren. He insists on keeping very close contact, getting photographs and that, and he paints and makes toys for the children. Martin, the oldest grandchild, has been visiting his grandfather since he was three weeks old.

'He still runs our lives from England. When he's writing he's always arranging everything. Hopefully when he's out I can sit back and relax and let him get on with it. I hope it'll return to how it was.'

But she admits she has changed. 'I wasn't independent at all. Brian made all the decisions. But I'm independent now. I've had to be. I wouldn't say I'm the same person I was when he went in. I'm a lot older and a lot wiser.'

Chrissie and Brian celebrated their twenty-fifth wedding anniversary in Leicester prison. 'Wedding anniversaries were always very special for us; we always went away or something. All the children had arranged a surprise party for me. They took me out for a meal. The whole family was there and they had a video made. When I went over to see him he'd done a painting of me.

'Then there was the thirtieth anniversary. It seemed no time since the twenty fifth. My daughter Bernadette was in Florida. I always have the morning visit alone, and the kids come in for the afternoon. Fifteen minutes into the afternoon visit the door opened and Bernadette walked in, all the way from Florida.

'But the best of it was, all the screws in the prison knew about it, they were all waiting, and they were all smiling when she arrived. The kids couldn't have given us a nicer present. Brian was annoyed about it afterwards — it was the only thing he hadn't arranged, something had happened and he wasn't in on it!'

The question of Brian being transferred to serve out the rest of his sentence close to home arose when she became ill a year ago. 'I have a chronic blood disorder. I was rushed into hospital last New Year's Day. It was touch and go for my kidneys. It was a very bad time for him. I had pneumonia and pleurisy, and he did try for a transfer. I said to him, even if I died in hospital there was no way they would have let him home. But he was so panic-stricken he tried. I didn't know till afterwards that he was very ill himself with a chest infection. He didn't get transferred, and generally I never thought about a transfer because I didn't expect them to send him home.

'I just count myself lucky that I'm able to go over on visits. Now with the illness if I don't feel well I don't go. The last time it was marvellous. We went by car and had none of the hassle with trains and bags and things. '

Chrissie is a quiet, dignified woman, and expresses no anger or bitterness about what has happened to her. She is reluctant to talk about their plans for Brian's release. 'He keeps talking about it. I say we'll think about it when the time comes. I suppose I have more to keep me going. I think at the back of my mind I'm afraid something might happen. We'll probably go away on our own, no one will know where. '

Irene

Where a prisoner is not married, or where the relationship has come to an end, another member of the family assumes the responsibility for maintaining contact. More often than not it is a woman.

Irene's brother Peter was arrested in June 1985, along with a number of others, and charged with conspiracy to cause explosions at a number of seaside resorts on specified dates. He was convicted and sentenced to life imprisonment, with a recommendation that he serve a minimum of twenty years. It is his third period of imprisonment for IRA activities.

Peter has two children, but his marriage had broken up before his last arrest and another relative takes the two children to see him. His mother is dead and his father is sixty-eight and frail; the journey would be too much for him. Irene and the relative who takes the children keep in touch with him.

'When I'm going on a visit I fly from Belfast to Heathrow, take a train from Waterloo to the coast and then a boat to the Isle of Wight. It takes ten to thirteen hours, depending on connections. It costs between £300 and £400 for three or four days and you get four or five visits in. If I'm sharing the visit with one of his friends I just go in for the afternoon visit.

'We get searched, but the prison officers are well-enough mannered. I'd be dressed to the nines, and I never wear the same outfit twice. They'll never be able to say the Irish are not well-dressed and well-mannered! The first visit is a bit difficult. It takes a while to settle into a conversation after not seeing him for a number of months. When that's over you settle in.

'We were always very close, though he's thirty five and I'm twenty three. I was only six when he went to jail first; he did about eleven years altogether. Now I'm getting to know him again. But it's very difficult. There's a partitioned room for two visitors at a time. There are two or three screws sitting beside the visitors. It's very inhibiting. You have to talk in a coded way to get intimate things across, and you hold back on certain personal things. It's not a question of keeping up a front for him; he's not the sort of person you can fool. He'd know straight away if something was wrong. The prison officers write everything down, what you are wearing, what the relationship seems to be with the prisoner, how you are getting on.

'You're so tensed up going in on a visit, and when you leave it's very, very emotional when he says, "When will I see you again?" I travel back up to London in knots, in a state of bewilderment. I'm in a bit of a downer for a few weeks afterwards. It's probably harder for Peter — me leaving him — he's so isolated compared with the prisoners over here. If he was transferred here it would be easier. Maybe next year there'll be changes in the review system in England.'

Liam

Some people are more stoical about their situation. Liam, from the Docks area of Belfast, was arrested in England in 1974 and sentenced to twenty years in prison for conspiring to cause an explosion. With normal remission he should be out by now, but he was sentenced to an additional four years for assault following a brawl with one of the Littlejohns (brothers jailed for activities they claimed they had carried out as British spies in the Official Republican movement) in Gartree. He also lost three years remission when he refused to wear prison clothes in protest at the body-searching of his mother, who was ill at the time, when she went to visit him. She died suddenly two years ago.

His sister Maura tries to keep in touch through letters and visits. A brother's wife and children visit every two years or so, as does Maura. This brother cannot visit himself, as he has been excluded from Britain under the PTA. 'I haven't seen my brother for sixteen years. It's very annoying,' he said. Another sister and cousins who are very close to them also visit. They all save up and try to spread the visits. An English woman friend of Liam's visits regularly.

'We all take turns as well as we can afford it,' said his brother, who did not want his name published. 'It's very, very difficult. I'm not working and our mother was a widow. My mother could claim help from the DHSS but no one really wants to; you have to tell them what you get for your breakfast.'

He expresses the attitude of many republicans to

He expresses the attitude of many republicans to imprisonment. 'It's part and parcel of the game. You have to be prepared to lose your liberty and your life. There's no point in crying about it afterwards.'

He felt that they should also be prepared to sacrifice personal relationships. 'A fellow around here wrote to his wife asking her not to bother coming over any more. He was being realistic. It's a very sensible attitude, and is taking the pressure off her. She might be very annoyed at that. But he's being very sensible.'

Was this man not very lonely now? 'Yes, I don't think he has anyone going in visiting now. But if a young fellow of twenty-four or twenty-five has a wife and young children and gets thirty years it's only realistic to say, "Forget it."'

Did this not lead to the isolation of the women? 'Oh, yes. Even when that fellow wrote to his wife telling her not to come back there are some people who don't believe it. They think she wants to go with other fellows. But Liam's girlfriend has stuck by him, though she's English. She comes here every year.

'He's in brilliant spirits, but if you ask him anything he just clams up. He got on OK with the other prisoners in Category A (*high security*), but he's off Category A now because he's just serving the sentence for assault. Now he's in with a lot of East Enders and he can relate to them because they come from an area like this.

'I think the repatriation campaign in the 1970s was a waste of time. A lot of time and money was put into it. The Brits have their hostages and they won't give them up. Maybe it should be attacked under the British system. The Irish government should try to have prisoners transferred to prisons nearer the families. They proved they could do something with Brian Keenan. They should have done something sooner on the Birmingham Six and the Guildford Four, (*the Irish government began to raise these cases in 1985*) and they should do something more about transfers.'

May

If wives, children and siblings have the hope that they will be reunited with a prisoner when he is released, this is often something that parents cannot share. They may be too old to expect to live until the release of their son (or daughter). If they are frail, imprisonment in Britain brings total separation.

May is an elegant, white-haired woman in her early seventies. Her house in a small red-brick street off the Falls Road is beautifully kept, and on a winter morning had a fire blazing in the grate. With Belfast hospitality she offered me lunch with her two grand-daughters who come there from school every day, part of the close family relationships which are a feature of life in that city. Her son Paul was arrested in Belfast in the house of a friend in 1984 and brought to England, where he was charged with causing explosions.

'When Paul was lifted Sister Sarah got in touch with us and met us at the airport when we went over and got us digs. She's a great person, but she's the world's worst bloody driver. She used to go the wrong way up one-way streets. The police would arrest her and when they saw she was a nun let her go. But she's been so good.'

Paul's trial came up seven months later. He did not plead and he received four life sentences with a recommendation that he serve thirty-five years. He was moved to Albany on the Isle of Wight.

It took May all day to get there to see him. Then he was transferred to Gartree outside Leicester, and she found it easier. 'I could fly to Birmingham, get the train to Leicester and then to Market Harbour and a taxi to the prison.

'The social welfare helps with the cost, including the flight, because I've got a doctor's certificate that I have to fly. They allow £10 for bed and breakfast and £3.15 a day for food. But you're always out. It's £18.50 a day for bed and breakfast in Full Sutton and you can't eat out for £3.15 a day. It's hard for a pensioner living alone. My daughters give me something towards it; otherwise I could not go. If I stopped going there's just one of my daughters would go. I have three other sons, one of them's in Australia, the other two don't bother. They can't

53

afford to get involved. There's no point in them going over and getting lifted in England.

'I used to be afraid of the PTA, but I don't care now. I was lifted one time and they kept me a full hour until they let me go when I said I was going to see my son in prison. When I told them they said, "We could have told you that."

'I had another son shot dead by the police in 1972. Paul was just coming up to sixteen. It got to the stage he couldn't go to school with the army looking for him. After Albert was killed we were getting raided day in and day out, and I wasn't surprised when he was lifted. I was surprised when he was taken to England, though.'

Before his arrest Paul was going out with Martina, who was one of his co-defendants in the trial and is now in Durham prison. In May 1989 they married in prison. 'We were all there for it. The prison was very good. They laid on a buffet. One of the screws took three rolls of film and gave them to me. They were very, very good. It was an L-shaped visiting room and there was no sign of a screw anywhere. They all stayed down the far end. It was a registry office wedding. Paul wouldn't have the padre near him.

'The marriage helps. They have the right to one phone call a month and they can write as often as they like. But they can't visit. They say that visits from the women's prison in Durham are too high risk.

'He's always in good form. When I read the sentence, I thought "If that was me, I'd poison myself." He said not to look at it like that, to take it from day to day.

'I was born in Glasgow. It wasn't a republican family as much as nationalist. None of the other members of the family got involved. But you've got to stick by your kids. I can't say I'm not going to visit him, I can't let him rot there. I wouldn't be human if I said that.

'My husband used to take fits of depression. He used to sit and cry. I had to carry the full burden. He never saw Paul after his arrest. His heart was too bad for the journey. He died two years ago. But someone from the family comes up every day to see me.

'If he was transferred it would be money saved every way: it's only fifty pence on the minibus to Maghaberry or the Kesh. If he got back here they would both be in the one prison. There's men and women in Maghaberry. He's put in for transfer every year and every year he's turned down. When I'm going over someone has to go with me because I've got bronchitis and I'm not allowed travel alone. I'm seventy-three. I won't be able to keep it up much longer. There's a case going to the European Court about the transfers, but I might be dead by then.'

Betty and Isobel

Betty and Isobel from Derry are the mother and sister of Martina, who was arrested in England at the same time as Paul. 'It was a shock,' said her mother Betty. 'She always went here, there and everywhere on her holidays. As far as I was concerned she was away on her holidays. She was arrested on the Saturday in England and I didn't know until the following Wednesday when one of the neighbours brought in a paper. Afterwards when I looked back I thought I must have been simple or something.

'Living in this area, the older population were always nationalists. Now the people are republicans. The kids saw an awful lot growing up. Martina was the only one of the family involved. She has her beliefs and I wouldn't take them away from her. I wouldn't try. They all have their beliefs.'

Isobel does a lot of the visiting. 'I leave on a Friday morning and take the train to Belfast, then get a taxi to the airport. That all costs £19.90. The ticket costs £147; I get an open one; it means if I miss the flight I don't lose the ticket. I arrive in London and take the tube to King's Cross, which costs another £2.50, and then get the train to Durham, which is £87 return. Then I have to get a taxi to the bed and breakfast, clean myself up, go out for something to eat. The next morning I'm at the prison for ten and I get an hour and a half visit. Then I go for lunch and come back for the afternoon visit. The whole thing costs about £500. Everyone in the family organises around the visits.'

Betty is totally preoccupied by what is happening to Martina. 'I know nothing about prisons, but I said to her, if you do nothing else walk up and down that cell, talk to yourself, sing to yourself, keep your mind active. She's in top form now; she's studying politics in the Open University.

'Before, the screws used to be in front of her on the visit, close by, and you could see the tension in her eyes. Now they're at the far end of the room and she has her back to them. You like to bring her in something on the visit, stockings or flowers or something. We buy all her clothes and her books.' She produced a recent photograph of Martina in prison, a pretty, blonde girl dressed in a brightly-coloured sweatshirt and jeans. 'I try and dress her in the best, keep her up in the style.'

Like May, Betty sees the marriage between Martina and Paul as the high point of their imprisonment, though it was not without problems. 'A few days before the wedding they told us only three members of the family would be allowed in. Then they said all the girls could go. I have seven girls. You should have seen the panic!

'In Full Sutton, where Paul was, they were very relaxed. They even let my Sharon in to help Martina get ready. They had a big spread prepared. Martina and Paul paid for it, but it was good. The screws stayed away at the end of the room.

'Martina was radiant. The family had bought the wedding dress and had got the bridesmaid's dress made. Paul was very nervous. We hadn't seen him at all since the arrest. Then on the way back with Christina and Sheena, Christina was arrested. She looks very like Martina.'

Like all the other Irish prisoners in Britain, Martina has applied for a transfer to a prison in Northern Ireland to be closer to her family. She has no family connections in Britain. 'Every three months or so she writes to the Home Office about a transfer. The same excuses come back time after time,' said Isobel.

'If she was here we could see her every week', added Betty. '£3.50 takes me up to Maghaberry. She hasn't seen anybody except the family since she was arrested. I'm sure she's sick looking at us. She should see young people. If she was here all her friends could go and see her. You can't expect them now, with what people have to go through to visit over there, and the expense! Here you just send out a visit pass. There is no vetting.

'She's been sentenced to life with no release date. There's a light at the end of the tunnel here' (*the review system leads to definite release dates*).

Betty was preparing to visit Martina just after Christmas. 'I went at Christmas before. She put her arms around me and wished me a Happy Christmas. I didn't stop crying from when I left the prison until I walked in here.'

When Betty leaves the room Isobel talks of her concern for her mother: 'We put in very bad years with me mammy. She wouldn't go out for about five years. If it was a good day she would say, "Martina's in a cell" and start crying. I still come up here some days and find her in bed crying. She and Martina have a birthday on the same day and they have the same nature. We're all very close, but Martina is especially close to her.

'Mother has a heart condition. We took her to the doctor and he said she was suffering from anxiety and there was nothing he could do. As she gets older the visits will get harder and that's bothering her. She lives in hope for the case coming up in Strasbourg. I'm not too optimistic. There have been too many false dawns.'

Catherine

Catherine's son John was arrested in 1976, charged with conspiracy to cause explosions, convicted and sentenced to twenty years in prison. He was also involved in the Littlejohn attack and sentenced to a further four years.

Unmarried, his main contact is with his mother, Catherine, who lives in North Dublin. But she has not visited him since he was on remand in Brixton, fourteen years ago. A bright, sharp-tongued woman in her sixties, even her son does not escape the barbs of pointed humour she directs at everyone, but especially at politicians. 'I have no time for politicians good, bad or indifferent. They must be power-hungry. They use people for their own ends.

'John discouraged visits because you have to put down all sorts of details. It would draw attention to the family and there was the possibility of intimidation. He won't take visits from anyone, even Sister Sarah. He's like Greta Garbo. He wants to be alone. (*She rolls her eyes and mimics Garbo*.) Anyway, what would I be going over for? We communicate with letters.'

His letters cover everything from international affairs to world literature. She rummages in a box for a particular letter from October last and reads it out: 'The situation in the Gulf goes on and on and on . . . What about the Palestine issue? . . . the massacre in Jerusalem? . . . The real reason for it (*the Gulf crisis*) is that the US wants to keep the Japs and the Germans in check.'

He moves on to comment on the Dublin Theatre Festival ('I have to tell him what's on in the festival and that') and then to instructions to his mother to learn French. 'Go for the reading first. You build up a vocabulary and then you're reading the great books in the original.' He then moves on to the questions of Korean and German unity, asking, 'What about Ireland?' and finishes with some comments on the greenhouse effect.

'All his letters are like that. We write and he tells me what he was reading and I tell him what I'm reading. He's only reading French and German now. He was never any good at languages in school! He was always a very happy-go-lucky sort of fellow. What will he do when he comes out? He'll just get on with life. He has three accountancy exams.'

Catherine's is just one of the families in the Republic affected by imprisonment in Britain. Many have made great sacrifices to keep in touch with their relative, as the Irish government, unlike that of Northern Ireland, gives no assistance to people making visits to prisons in Britain. The total cost of a trip from, say, the west of Ireland, can amount to £1,000 and involve the whole family saving for one visit a year.

Under the Council of Europe Convention on the Transfer of Sentenced Prisoners a prisoner may be transferred to his home state if the state holding the prisoner and the state receiving him agree. However, while Ireland has signed the Convention the government has not ratified it, so Irish prisoners in Britain cannot apply for transfer here. When asked about this, the Department of Justice expressed the fear that it would lead to a rush of applications which would flood the already overcrowded prison system. However, the Irish Commission for Prisoners Overseas estimates that less than forty political prisoners would apply initially, with the figure levelling off at less than ten a year. Discussions continue between organisations like the ICPO and the Department.

Jim and Carmel

Jim and Carmel also live in Dublin, though Jim comes from the North. They moved down South in the late 1970s after both Jim and his brother Joe were arrested during Operation Motorman in 1972. Joe travelled home regularly to see to the family farm, and on one of those trips, in 1986, he was arrested and taken to Paddington Green police station in London and questioned 'in connection with explosions on the mainland'. Specific explosions were mentioned, but when he came to trial in the spring of 1987 the charges had been changed to conspiracy to cause explosions. He pleaded guilty to one, lesser, charge, claiming he was working for his brother in the latter's electronics firm, to explain his fingerprint on a timing device. The jury brought in a majority guilty verdict on all the charges, and he was sentenced to sixteen years imprisonment which the judge described as 'lenient' because of his age. He was sixty-one.

Joe is unmarried, and his sister-in-law, Carmel, was the only member of the family cleared to visit him at first. One by one her children applied and received permission to visit him, and someone now visits him three times a year, flying in the winter and travelling by boat and train in the summer. Jim fears arrest in Britain and cannot visit him. 'He's dead as far as I'm concerned. '

'At the moment his release date is 6 January 1997. That's a long time away when you're sixty-five' said Carmel. 'He has high blood pressure and poor eyesight. It's a bad place to grow old. He started an Open University course, but his eyes were failing and he had to give it up. He writes long letters home. They're political epistles twelve or fourteen pages long.'

Jim and Carmel are angry with the Dublin government for its lack of sympathy and support. 'We're harassed here. Joe worked for years here with the Department of Agriculture and the

Special Branch tried to get him out of his job. Since he went to jail they called to the girlfriend of our son Paul and told her not to have anything to do with the family, and that they would hassle her if she did. It happened to another son recently. This whole thing is affecting another generation. I've been to TDs about it and they say, "What do you expect?" You're termed a terrorist and you've no civil rights.'

Joe, like most of the other prisoners, has applied for a transfer to Northern Ireland, which would bring him nearer his family. His request was refused in September 1990 in a letter which said: 'In view of the seriousness of the crimes you were convicted of it would not be appropriate for you to benefit from the substantial reduction of the sentence you have to serve which would be a consequence of your transfer to Northern Ireland.'

Making the Case for Transfer

Not only the prisoners in Britain and their families, but a wide range of organisations associated with prisoners' welfare, have urged the Home Office to consider granting Irish prisoners' requests to be transferred to Northern Ireland.

One such organisation is the British-based National Association of Prison Officers. In a press statement on 24 February 1987 the general secretary of NAPO, Harry Fletcher, said: 'The call for transfer is based on humanitarian grounds. There is considerable pressure on the families of the prisoners because of the emotional stress and journeys involved. Many relatives, particularly the elderly and children, cannot visit. This places additional strain on prisoners and exacerbates control problems for the authorities.'

In a letter to the then Home Secretary, Douglas Hurd, he pointed out that the Northern Ireland Association for the Care and Resettlement of Offenders (NIACRO) and the Irish Commission for Prisoners Overseas both supported transfer. NIACRO had said: 'It seems ludicrous, considering the overcrowding in British prisons and the comparative space in the prisons here, that the authorities do not arrange transfers automatically.' The ICPO added: 'The isolation and breakdown of family ties and contact experienced by prisoners and their families is multiplied in the case of prisoners overseas.'

NAPO went on to answer the arguments against transfer made by the Home Office. 'The Home Office has argued that transfer would provoke public anxiety. NAPO believes that the transfer would relieve public anxiety in England and Wales because the prisoners would be housed elsewhere. Transfer is unlikely to heighten anxiety in Northern Ireland because the grounds for transfer were humanitarian and not political and because of the numbers already held in Irish prisons.

'The Northern Ireland Office has stated that the prisoners would be regarded as heroes and this would diminish the deterrent value of punishment. NAPO believes that the prisoners transferred from England and Wales would be unlikely to become important figures in a system which detains hundreds of people convicted of similar offences.

'The Northern Ireland Office has been of the view that transfer would strain the system and endanger security. NAPO believes that the total number of category 'A' prisoners transferred would be around forty, and other categories less than three hundred. They would therefore not place a large strain on the prison system. In any event a new top security prison for four hundred prisoners at Maghaberry, County Antrim, has recently been opened. However, on 20 January 1987 the male population of the prison was eleven.

'The Home Office has felt that transfer would reduce the possibility of terrorists severing links with paramilitary organisations. NAPO believes that the present system in England and Wales of isolating Irish prisoners individually or in small groups in high security dispersal prisons causes as much bitterness as incarceration in the H-blocks of Northern Ireland. There is little doubt that dedicated prisoners who believe in their cause will not break their links with paramilitary organisations by enforced separation from their families.

'Both the Northern Ireland Office and the Home Office have argued that prisoners after transfer would benefit from higher remission allowed in Northern Ireland. NAPO believes that the numbers affected by higher remissions are very small and whilst numbers affected by higher remissions are very small and whilst they may benefit from an earlier release if serving a determinate sentence they would be subject to conditional release licence and therefore would, if convicted of a further offence during the licence period, serve the balance of the original sentence.'

Since this letter NIACRO has learned that the Northern Ireland Office no longer opposes transfer, and the opposition is now centred in the Home Office. The last point made in the NAPO letter is the one most often cited by the Home Office in its recent replies to requests for transfer, but this is no longer valid since the change in remission regulations in Northern Ireland. Yet no transfers have been allowed since then.

I sought a meeting with a spokesperson for the Home Office to discuss its policy on the matter, sending the request in writing with the dates I would be in London. While in London, a message came from the Home Office to *The Irish Times* office there that the official I needed to speak to would not be available that week. When I asked if there was any other official who would be in a position to discuss the matter of transfer I was told there was not. I then asked when the official who was informed on this issue would be available, as I could come back to London and talk to her, and was told she would not become available at any stage.

The Labour Party's spokesman on Northern Ireland is Kevin MacNamara, who would expect to become Secretary of State for Northern Ireland in the event of a Labour victory in the next election. He was much more forthcoming about the question: 'The basic principle is that it is the individual who commits the crime and not the family. Yet the families suffer. So as a general principle where the person serves their sentence would be where that does least damage to their near and dear. If the crime is committed in the UK I see no problem with transfer to Northern Ireland. That general principle is no problem for the British Labour Party. What mustn't happen is that the family suffers because of the actions of the father or mother, son or daughter.'

Reactions from the families to his statement have been mixed. Some spoke contemptuously of the record of the British Labour party, when in power, on questions like the Prevention of

Terrorism Act. Others grasped gratefully at any straw of hope that their relative might be brought to serve their sentence within easy reach of visits.

Meanwhile Gareth Peirce is taking a case on behalf of a number of named prisoners to the European Court of Human Rights, citing articles 8 and 14 of the European Convention, one of which guarantees the right to family life and the other opposes discrimination on the grounds of politics, national or social origin. But this case is unlikely to be heard for over a year.

Chapter Two

Double Victims: Coping with Miscarriages of Justice

If the time lost by the Guildford Four, the Birmingham Six and the Maguire Seven as a result of miscarriages of justice in Britain in the 1970s were added up, the figure would come to over two hundred years. These sentences affected a great number of people. In the case of the Birmingham Six, the BBC *Everyman* programme counted the immediate relatives, the wives, children and grandchildren alone, as seventy six. The men also had parents, brothers, sisters and other close relatives who became involved. Equally, dozens of people were affected by the victimisation of the Guildford Four and the Maguire Seven.

When these people were sentenced their families were condemned to years of separation, stress and isolation. Two of the marriages of the Birmingham Six broke up. One woman, Sarah Conlon, lost her husband who died in prison due to the lack of care needed for the long-term illness from which he suffered. Her sister-in-law, arrested at the same time and released without charge, lost her appetite and her health and has not eaten a solid meal since. Families suffered attacks from hostile gangs and had to move from their homes.

In many ways they suffered more than the families of those who do not deny their involvement in the activities for which they were convicted. Many of these people lived in England and had no contact with the republican movement, so they lacked the support and solidarity enjoyed by the families of republican prisoners in the nationalist communities in Northern Ireland. They abhorred the crimes for which their husbands, sons and fathers had been sentenced, and wanted passionately to prove their innocence and obtain their release. Yet when they knocked on the doors of priests, politicians and public figures seeking support for their campaign, they were met with disbelief or indifference. Almost two decades later, many of them still bear the scars of those years.

Sarah Conlon

Sarah Conlon is still grieving for Giuseppe, ten years after his death in prison. For her the nightmare of the wrongful conviction of her family for the Guildford bombings did not end with the release of her son, Gerry, in October 1989 after fifteen years in prison.

She is still a good-looking woman, neatly dressed as she sits in her well-kept home near St Peter's Cathedral in West Belfast. But she is very sad and rarely smiles. Tears come to her eyes frequently as she talks softly and fluently about the years of suffering while her husband and son were in jail.

'I had a good husband. He should be here with me now. It just seemed they took part of my life away. I know what they put me through. They wrecked my life completely. Most people think it's alright now with Gerry being out, but you won't forget the hard years that you've been through. Thanks be to God I never held any bitterness. But it'll never leave my mind.'

She felt completely isolated for years, without even the support given to families of members of the IRA by support organisations. As her family had nothing to do with the IRA she could not have and did not want any moral or financial support from organisations linked to them.

'Who was I? I was nobody. The only two friends I had were Sister Sarah Clarke and Father Faul. Sister Sarah believed in their innocence. Everyone else closed their door. They thought I was IRA and didn't want to get involved'.

The memory of the visits haunts her. A quiet, dignified woman, she shrank from the attention her situation attracted and constantly feared some kind of attack, verbal or physical. 'We put in a very bad time with the visits. I always had to take one of my two daughters with me. I would never travel over to England alone. My husband travelled alone and I could never forget what

65

happened to him.

'If it had been the case that they were guilty, as a wife and mother I would have done my duty and gone to visit. But the thing that hurt me terribly was knowing they shouldn't even be there. When you've been through these things yourself you know what other people have to suffer. I pray every day for the Birmingham Six and all the other prisoners wrongly convicted. God help anyone over there who doesn't have anyone to visit them. We used to get the boat to Stranraer and then got the London coach, which stopped at Birmingham. We sat in Digbeth station from a quarter to four in the morning until ten to seven to get the bus to the prison, arriving at half past nine. We would never have a taste of water to wash our faces from five the previous evening leaving Belfast. Then Digbeth closed for renovations and we were afraid to go into New Street station. There were drunk men there; you were sitting on a bench with your daughter and grandchildren, and these would be sitting on the other benches. Things would go through your head . . . I had a bad time even from bus drivers. Once I asked a driver on the way up to the prison on a Friday if this was the last bus from Birmingham and he said, "Why, are you going up to see one of the IRA bombers?" Then the Saturday morning, it was the last visit of the series, I had the buggy and my daughter had the baby in her arms, and the same driver came by with just two people on the bus. He went past us, and Bridie (my daughter) had to get a taxi. Through all that I was late for my visit.'

She experienced what can only be described as vindictiveness on the part of the prison authorities and some prison officers. 'Once I was going to see Gerry and Giuseppe, God rest him, in Wakefield. I got there and they told me that my son had been moved that morning to Canterbury. We had written to them and given them ample notice of the visit. It meant I had only four days in Wakefield. I stood at the top of Love's Lane and just sat down in the rain. Then I got up and went to the chapel and asked the priest could he recommend a place to stop. He told me of a B and B: it cost £13.'

Because she was working as an orderly in the Royal Victoria Hospital, she was not eligible for the social security assistance available for visits to those on social welfare and had to save hard for the money for the visits. 'If I had the money it cost me over the years I could sit back and forget about work. For seventeen years I was working with women and girls up in the hospital and at the tea-breaks they'd talk about going on holidays to Spain and Italy and that, and I'd think to myself, "You know where you're going — to visit prisons."

'The strip-searches were the worst. You got headaches that you thought you'd never get rid of. You had to sit waiting on the lady searchers coming, and everyone was looking at you as if you were a criminal. It was very, very degrading. Then you were told, "Sorry, they're late this morning." It cut a half-hour off your visit. The attitude was, they were IRA bombers and even if you arrived early they would leave you till last. Giuseppe refused a visit once because of what I had to go through.'

She felt overwhelmed by hostility everywhere she went, fearing that her accent and the knowledge of where she was going would open her to attack. 'I would have given the world for a cup of tea many a time, but I was afraid to go in anywhere and ask for a cup of tea. You felt people's eyes going through you. Whenever you were over there you were afraid you would not get home safe.'

However, her biggest grief is not for her suffering, but for Giuseppe. Although he is dead ten years, tears often come into her eyes as she speaks of him. 'When I'd done the visit all I could do on the way home was sit and cry, seeing him between two men and big Alsatian dogs. It was just something on your mind when you woke up in the morning. It's still with me.

'I'll never forget what they did to him. After the 1979 riot in Wakefield they beat all the prisoners except him because he was so sick, but they wrecked his cell, and tore up the photos of the grandchildren and me.

'Gerry and Giuseppe were not here to see the girls getting married and he isn't here to see his grandchildren grow up. They would not even let him have Christmas cards if they were anyway padded. He never got them. I got them all back when he died.

'On one visit, I asked the prison officer in the morning if I could bring him in a piece of fruit in the afternoon. He said, No, that was a luxury. I said it was a necessity in his state of health, and he agreed.

'Then there was the afternoon visit, and the partition was between us as usual. I handed a pear over it to Guiseppe. He always loved a pear. One of the prison officers jumped up and pulled it out of his mouth. I said to him, "I got permission" but Giuseppe said, "Leave it." I told the prison officer if he ever ate a pear he should remember what he did to a sick man. The things they did I could not do to my worst enemy. I'll never forget what they did to Giuseppe.'

Like many other Irish prisoners, Giuseppe and Gerry Conlon sought transfer to prison in Northern Ireland. They were refused. 'If he was here he'd be in the Kesh or Crumlin Road. His family would have been able to see him once a fortnight. We could bring in parcels. I used to imagine if they were transferred over here, it'd be like them being free.

'The governor of Wormwood Scrubbs sent for me one day and said, "Mrs Conlon, I know your husband's innocent. I'm on the phone every day to Whitelaw saying his health is deteriorating".' But these representations did no good, and Giuseppe Conlon's health continued to worsen.

'At the end they brought him to Hammersmith Hospital. After a while there it was getting so that he could eat presentable food. Then they took him out of it on one of the coldest days in January. (*The hospital had been told of rumours of a planned rescue attempt by the IRA. No evidence of any such bid has ever been found.*)

'I wouldn't have believed it if I didn't see it with my own eyes. A priest who said he knew he was innocent let them do that. I never knew such coldness as in Hammersmith Hospital. It killed me coming away from that last visit.'

She was still hopeful that he would be released on parole, given the state of his health, so when her sister and brother-in-law came to the hospital where she worked nine or ten days after that visit she thought they had been phoned with news of his release. Instead they brought the news of his death in prison.

'I'd had a wee bit of a letter from him wishing me a happy

birthday — my birthday was on 20 January — and asking me to excuse his writing, he was not getting any better; he was getting worse. He died on the 23rd, on Wednesday just before seven o'clock. We didn't get his remains till eleven o'clock on Sunday.

'They said they could bury him in the prison grounds. Oh God, he was there when he was alive. I wasn't going to leave him there after he died. I was going to bring him home. He's up in Milltown (*cemetery*) now. I was up there last Sunday.

'British Airways wouldn't fly him home. They said he was a terrorist, and Aer Lingus had to fly him to Dublin. They took £933 from me to get Giuseppe's remains home. I have the bill here. I have Gerry's wages here too, £34.90 for fifteen years.

'Then there was Hugh and Kate (*her brother and sister-in-law*) counting up every penny, working year after year just to save up to go to prisons they should never have been going to.' Hugh and Kate Maguire were the only members of the family in England not to be jailed, and they visited the Conlons and the Maguires regularly.

'I used to ask God every day that their innocence would be proved. It will always be a miracle to me that it happened. I knew they were innocent and God knew they were innocent. I would not say I was ever very religious, but I always had faith in God. If I didn't have God I'd have had no one to turn to.

'The good thing is, Gerry's out. The sad thing is, Giuseppe came out in a coffin. I still wake up in the morning thinking "our Gerry's out." I wish Giuseppe was with him, but I know he would not change places. He was a good man. We had a good marriage. He'd have loved to have seven grandchildren.'

Sarah Conlon's daughters live near her, and they and their husbands and children are often in the house. Surely this prevents her from being lonely?

'They're married now, and their husbands and children come first, naturally. And I wouldn't like Gerry to settle down in Belfast. Sometimes you feel that loneliness. If Giuseppe was here it would have been he and I together.'

69

Hugh and Kate Maguire

The arrest of Gerry Conlon and Paul Hill of the Guildford Four led to the arrest of Gerry's aunt, Annie Maguire, and her family, and his father, Giuseppe Conlon, who had come over to help his son and was staying with the Maguires. Another aunt and uncle, Hugh and Kate Maguire, were also arrested, but, unlike the others, they were later released without charge. However, they also paid heavily for the Guildford bombings.

Hugh is a humorous, ebullient Belfastman — 'I still have a bet, a drink, and go out with my mates to play cards.' He recalls what happened. 'It was a Friday night. We went to bed early. Then there was an unmerciful pounding on the door. I opened it and saw a crowd there. I never saw so many. I counted seventeen armed policemen in the flat, and there was a policewoman, uniformed police and sniffer dogs. They never questioned me about Gerry; they asked me about my brother Paddy. Then they put me in a Panda car and brought me to Paddington Green police station. I saw Kate there. She'd been taken there before me.

'We were put in a bus with other people and taken to Guildford, where we were photographed and fingerprinted, etc. They refused me a drink. I had ulcerated legs and I went from Saturday to Saturday without any treatment. I had just had an operation to remove my kneecap and they kept me three days and four nights without a blanket or a mattress, in the dead of winter. I was only questioned once about did I belong to any organisation.

'The degrading thing about it was I could not wash or shave or see a doctor. I had no bedding and no mattress. Then they released us, and asked us how we were getting home. They said, "We'll drive you all the way to London." I said, "You will not." They said, "I advise you to cover your faces; there's a crowd outside." We were stupid, we did.

'They took me to Paddington Green first,' said Kate. 'We never wet our lips from when we left here on the Friday until we got a cup of tea on Sunday. They put me in a cell on my own with a toilet in it. They took my shoes and tights. I used to wash the soles of my feet and my underpants in the flush of the toilet (*she was having her period at the time*). I had no comb, nothing. They really degraded you.

'I was handcuffed and taken to an interview room a few feet away. I was interrogated, interrogated — "Come on, Kate, tell us everything." I was supposed to be seen running from the pub. I said I was never in this place (*Guildford*) in my life.

'I was on the change of life at the time and I didn't know it. I got it very early. I was on this bunk bed and there was an awful smell in the room. I was as weak as water. I was brought out for exercise and I got dizzy. I have false teeth and I took them out and I was such a bundle of nerves I broke them.

'I took nothing to eat at all while I was in there. That's how I lost my appetite.' Kate has not eaten anything solid since her arrest seventeen years ago. She drinks tea and gets nourishment from Complan and vitamins. 'She's an advertisement for Complan. She's lived on it for seventeen years, ' Hugh said.

She was preoccupied with what was happening to Hugh and worried about his leg. When she asked her interrogators about him they told her he had been deported. 'They were really trying to break me. I don't know what they were trying to break me for.'

Eventually she was brought to see Hugh and they were released together. 'You should have seen the state of Hugh. I thought I was bad until I saw him. His beard was down to here. I asked him if they had looked after his leg, and he said no. When we got out he said, "We'll ring Paddy (*Annie Maguire's husband and his brother*) and say we're out." Jesus Christ, that was only the beginning of it. It was so sad. We thought Paddy and them would be here when we phoned up. Someone said they'd all been arrested. We never even knew Giuseppe was in London. Oh my God . . .' She covered her face in her hands. Again and again in the interview it is what happened to the others, not to herself, that upsets her most.

'I used to cry when I left him after a visit. He couldn't walk, he couldn't breathe. I was the last person to see Giuseppe Conlon alive. I was there the day he said to Gerry, "I want you to clear my name." God love him.'

Hugh used to travel around the country visiting all the members of the family who were in prison: 'I used to leave here on a Monday morning with a bag. I'd go to Durham to see Annie, then to Wakefield to see Paddy and Giuseppe, then to Aylesbury to see the two Maguire boys. Gerry was on the Isle of Wight. It was an awful lot of travelling.'

Kate explained how her health was affected by her experience. 'I was working at the time we were arrested. Afterwards I could not go out to work for a week, I was so nervous. See that standard lamp? I used to take that into the kitchen to cook. I used to say to Hugh, "If they don't see any light they won't come and take us." I couldn't answer the phone for months. I'm still nervous in this house, you know.

'I used to be always crying, crying, crying for them in prison. I had to go to my doctor. I was going to have a nervous breakdown. He put me on a week's tranquillisers. I was working as a cleaner in a pub at the time. They were nice people. They took me out of it. I was in a bad state. I used to sit like that (*she picked at her hands in her lap*). I just kept on drinking tea. They said I couldn't live like that, drinking tea, tea. I ate something and threw it up. That's how I found out I couldn't eat.

'The doctor said to take Complan, plenty of it. I take it once a day. A specialist came in to where Hugh used to work, and he told him about me, and the specialist said to take vitamins. If I go to Belfast and they put a dinner in front of me I have to go to the toilet and . . . you know. It doesn't go down to my stomach. It sits here in my chest. All I do is smoke and drink tea. I don't drink anything else at all. I don't even bother going out. I used to love going out. We heard the news of Gerry's release on a news flash and we did go out that night. I was not drinking, but Hugh was.

'We go on holidays, but we always go self-catering because I don't eat. I take the Complan everywhere. I'm so nervous now. When the two Bristol police came down here (*for the inquiry into the investigation of the Guildford case*) Gareth Peirce had to tell them I was nervous and would be crying.

'It's terrible what Irish people had to go through. They always seemed to get the wrong people. I don't know how.'

Kate and Hugh may be compensated when the inquiry into the Guildford Four and Maguire Seven convictions is finally concluded. But nothing can bring back the capacity to take food, to go out and enjoy a drink with her husband and friends, to feel safe and comfortable in her own home, that she lost seventeen years ago because she was related to someone who was suspected, wrongly, of bombing a pub in Guildford.

Brian and Lily Kelly

Brian and Lily Kelly are also related to a victim of a miscarriage of justice, John Walker of the Birmingham Six, but they escaped the worst of the experiences. They lived all their lives in Derry, and were there when they learned of the arrest of John, Lily's brother.

'Teresa (*John's wife*) had to leave Birmingham and she came to me,' said Lily. 'Brian got her fixed up in a house. I went over to see John in April, six months after his arrest. He was in Winson Green (*remand prison*) on remand. I was never in England in my life. I was never in a prison in my life and I was shaking. I said I wanted to visit John Walker, and they said "The Walker?" I said, "That's right." I was put in a room with a woman who turned out to be Eileen Callaghan (*married to another of the Birmingham Six*).

'Then I was taken into a small room and John was brought in. He looked like an old man. He started to cry when he saw me. He said, "I want the people in Derry and back home, especially my aunts, to know I had nothing to do with it. I don't care what other people believe."

'I was there for a week, and each day he got brighter and brighter. He had seen no one yet. Teresa was here. I went over two or three times a year after that. Then Brian started going over.

'Wakefield was horrible. I don't know exactly where it is. All I know is when I was in England I was travelling constantly, starting with getting a train from here to Belfast, then a plane to Birmingham.'

Lily, a warm and cheerful woman, thinks that something positive came out of John's imprisonment. 'When I go to visit John it's as if I never left him, we're so close. I was at the (*1987*)

73

appeal for the second week, with Skuse and them. When I came in John looked up and saw me. You should have seen his face! It broke my heart to see him sitting there. I think it has brought us closer together as a family. We all stand behind the prisoners here. If he had stayed just living in England we would have met maybe every ten years. He's said himself that one good thing came out of it all, his family moved to Ireland. The community cares for a prisoner's family here.

'My mother died when John was ten and I was four. My granny and two aunts raised us. Our aunts are eighty and eighty-two now. They're just waiting for John to get out, he's just hoping to get out before they die.'

Lily's story is typical of that of many families in the North. 'Our family was never republican before these troubles. I remember going down on those civil rights marches and saying to Brian, "We're doing this for our kids, that they won't have to put up with what we did." Then after John's arrest I went to Bishop Daly and John Hume and all them. They didn't want to know. Yes, I am bitter about it. The Bishop and I were very great, but he never mentioned John's name to me afterwards. I'm a republican now.'

So is her son Adrian. A champion schoolboy swimmer, he was not even in his teens when his uncle was jailed. Nine years later he was arrested, charged with the murder of a policeman, convicted and sentenced to life imprisonment. According to Lily, one of the first things John Walker is going to do when he is released, is go and visit his nephew in Long Kesh.

Teresa and Veronica Walker

John's wife is the only one of the wives of the Birmingham Six to leave England, where they were all living at the time of their arrest, and return to Ireland. It was John's idea, according to Teresa: 'I went to see him in Winson Green after he was arrested, and he was very badly beaten. He told us to come back here to his sister Lily. We came back on 4 December. I didn't believe he was guilty. I thought it was all a big mistake and he would come home after the trial, but he didn't. After that we were going backwards and forwards on visits, taking a few of the young ones with me each time. I moved back to England for a while so that we could visit more often. The young ones could not cope, so I sold up and came back here. I wouldn't leave here now. Most of the rest of the families will have to move when the men get out, but we won't. We're all settled here. The neighbours will do the whole street up with bunting and all when he's released.'

John's arrest made a big difference to the family's standard of living. 'Before that Mum, Dad and Bernie were all working, so we had good wages coming into the house,' said Veronica, her eldest daughter. 'I never went back to work; it was impossible,' said Teresa. 'It was just like changing your life. One day your husband gets arrested and everyone hates you. The first Christmas was the worst. We didn't even celebrate it.'

Veronica was fifteen when her father was arrested. 'I had a father for fifteen years, then he was gone. It was hard that way. I didn't see him until about a year after his arrest. I go four or five times a year now.' Her sister Dawn was little more than a baby. 'I don't remember his arrest. I vaguely remember going to Kellys, and growing up in the Bogside. We had a wee flat there first. I can only ever remember seeing him in prison. You got to realise that was your father. We always sent him our school reports and all. He always made you know he's your father. Being in jail made no difference to that.

'Even though he wasn't here, he would still get on to you about things, like "Don't you be coming in late." Mother would write and tell him everything. She'd say, "He's still your father. He should know what you're doing."

'He phones on special occasions like marriages, Christmas, birthdays and the births of children,' said Teresa. 'He worries more about us, because we're so far away. I'll be glad when he comes home and it all settles down. All he wants to do when he gets out is take the gran'wains to the beach. He has no great plans, just to be with his family.'

Last November there was still no sign of when this might be though the Walkers had to wait only another four months. 'They just build up your hopes and let you down,' said Veronica, 'but you get used to it after the years.' They have no illusions that it will all be plain sailing. 'It's going to be hard enough having a father around again, having a man about the house.'

Sandra Hunter

Sandra Hunter was born and reared in Birmingham and married Gerry Hunter when she was seventeen. She had three children by the time she was twenty. A few years later disaster struck. 'I was twenty five when I lost him. Our twenty-fifth wedding anniversary is next year.'

Her house was attacked and wrecked and she fled with her family to Gerry's family in Belfast. 'I looked at those streets, the kerb stones painted, the graffiti, the British soldiers, and I thought, "I've got to get out of here. I don't want to lose my kids to the troubles, as I have already lost Gerry." I said to Kate McIlkenny (*who had also moved back*). "I'm going back. We can't fight it from over here. It happened over there. I'm going next weekend." She said, "If you are, I'm going with you."

'I came back and stayed with my brother. The house had been wrecked, the three-piece was slashed, the walls were daubed, everything was stolen. Eventually I got a house from the council. The neighbours here don't know who I am. (*Sandra uses her maiden name.*) A few do. They're lovely, but most think I'm divorced. I never said I was, they just think that. I'm just Sandra to them. The fear has gone now, but it took years to go. In the 1970s I was petrified. You can run on your own but you can't run with three babies.'

However, Sandra is reluctant to talk about those years. 'I don't want to look back. I want to look forward. When you look back it's sad. No one wants to look back. We're on a high expecting them to get out. We'll have to come down when it's all over. We'll have to get it out of our system once and for all. It will be quite a harrowing time. It's quite frightening to think about.

'You'll sit up in a court and your whole life changes — again! You're going to go "Whoof" again. It makes me quite angry. If you kill someone you get built up for your release for five years with counselling and home leave and that. If you're innocent they throw you out with nothing.

'Till the day you die you'll be wondering what would it be like if it hadn't happened. How many kids would you have had? What would their names be? One of the kids said to me the other day, "Wouldn't it be great to have some money and to say, I'm going down the pub with my Dad?" I looked at him and thought, "You bastards, what right had you to take these things away from these kids?"

'I asked Gerry what he missed most of all, and he said, "I never saw my kids in a school uniform." When I thought of all the times I scraped to get Tracy a new dress to go up and visit him. . . He never saw his kids kick a ball. Both he and the boys are football-barmy.

'Some of the kids have a total blockage about what happened. One of them doesn't remember anything that happened before his dad was put away, and he was seven when it happened. He only remembers his dad in prison. When we talk about it he just looks blank. He didn't want to look at the horror; he didn't understand it. Yet he's always been a complete and utter brick to me, doing milk rounds and that. The kids were never in any trouble, except Gerry once got drunk on his birthday and was done for affray. I talked to them recently about all that and they said they kept out of trouble because they wouldn't bring the police to the house.'

Like the other women, she had to change when Gerry was jailed. 'I was always very dependent on Gerry, I couldn't even change a light bulb. When they sentenced him I thought I was going to die. I would rather have him go off with another woman; you'd know where you were then. I had no friends and hardly any family. I gradually came to terms with it. They wrecked my house and stole what they didn't wreck and I had to go to the council for another house. I did everything in this house myself. I made a home for the kids.

'Gerry doesn't know any different than looking after me. I'm a survivor now; it's a massive problem for him. We have so many arguments, there are so many bust-ups in prison. I say, "Don't you tell me what to do." In an argument last year he said, "I love you Sandra, but I don't like you." I looked at him and I said, "You've got it in one."

'I'm telling the other wives, it'll be a nightmare all over again when they get out. It's like getting together with a stranger. You learn to shy away from feelings when he has to go back to his cell. The closeness is there but you can't show it. But even if we split, I'll always love Gerry Hunter.'

However, when he was released in March 1991 and they spoke to journalists, their easy banter was testimony of the closeness which had endured.

Maggie McIlkenny

When the Birmingham Six won their appeal in March 1991 and emerged triumphant from the Old Bailey in London to greet the waiting press, one of the questions they were asked was how they survived almost seventeen years in prison and emerged so obviously sane. They all paid tribute to their families, and it was their families who not only sustained them, but who campaigned for them from the first years when no one wanted to know the Birmingham bombers. Every door was closed to those whose husbands, people thought, had committed the biggest mass murder in British legal history.

For the first ten years or so it was the wives who trudged from prison to prison, from public figure to public figure, placing the facts of the case before politicians and churchmen in the hope they would see what was wrong with it. Eventually, following the pamphlet of Fathers Denis Faul and Raymond Murray which aroused the interest of human rights campaigners in the United States of America, English journalist Chris Mullin took up the case and persuaded the Granada television programme *World in Action* to follow it up. That was the beginning of the end of their ordeal, though it was to last almost another six years.

By now most of the men's children were grown up, or growing up very fast. While they all had visited their fathers throughout their imprisonment, some of them now began to take up the task of publicly fighting for their release.

One of these was Maggie McIlkenny, the second youngest of Richard McIlkenny's six children, who spoke to me about her involvement in the campaign during the week in which the men were finally released following their second appeal.

Her introduction to public life happened almost by accident. 'One day there was this public meeting, and my mum asked me if I'd speak at it. At first I said no, then I agreed. I was visibly shaking and I had sweaty palms, I was so nervous. Then someone told me there was a prison warden sitting in the front row. I was so mad, I just spoke. There were about 300 people there; it was a Trades Council meeting. At the end I got a standing ovation and they voted to affiliate to the campaign and to provide an office. After that I just kept on, and now I just get on with it.'

Having her father in jail for something he didn't do affected everything in Maggie's life. 'We've always spoken as if he was there though he wasn't. We were always talking about my dad in the house. He was always part of my life.

'I was only eight when it all happened. It was terrible. The closest person to me in my life was suddenly taken away. I haven't ever come to terms with it. I won't until I hear the words saying he's totally exonerated.

'I school I put on a front. I used to beat people up, though I didn't realise why I did it. I didn't have many friends, I didn't want to mix. It affected me the way I'd socialise. I didn't really go around with boys, just my husband. I wouldn't have got married if my dad wasn't in jail, and I wouldn't have had kids early (*she has two daughters though she now regrets her marriage*). I'm not the marrying kind.

'I grew up in a house dominated by a woman, mainly made up of women (*she has one brother*). I find it hard to have a relationship with a man except friendship.'

She has a very strong relationship with her father. 'I idolise my dad, more than any man on this earth. He's always telling me he loves me. I think I've a better relationship with him than a lot of people do with dads living in the house.'

Yet she did not discuss day to day things like school work with him. 'I didn't want to pressure him with school work and that. It would be painful; he was not part of it though I would have loved him to be. I'd talk to him about people he knew and that. Going to visit my dad I'd always look my best so as not to let him worry.'

Maggie became one of the best known of the campaigners for the Birmingham Six, speaking frequently at public meeting, appearing on television chat shows, giving interviews to the press at every twist and turn of the case over the past five years. She and other members of the families, like her mother Kate McIlkenny, or Breda Power, became adept at dealing with lawyers, politicians, the media and, indeed, diplomats at international conferences.

'It was anger brought me into the campaign, watching the rest of the family hurting, watching my mother alone all those years, and she's tried so hard to keep the candle burning. It's affected my whole life. Now it just seems I've always been campaigning. Some good things have come of it, seeing how the judicial system works and that. But there were a lot of bad things, and those seventeen years can never be brought back.

'There is a lot of stress in it. I don't know how I'll react when it's all over. People expect you to speak, but they don't ask you how are you. I hate the limelight. I hate the responsibility of it. Everybody hangs on every word you say.

'But I don't think I would settle down to a nine to five job now. I'd like to help other people in prison who don't have families, people who've got too long sentences, or who've been wrongfully imprisoned. And I want my girls to understand, not to take things for granted. I want them to appreciate things, to appreciate people and not to be materialistic.'

She admitted to feeling very uncertain about the future on the eve of her father's release. 'It'll be different when the men are released. It'll be easier to talk about it. You only heal when you talk.

'In a way I'm a campaigner with a high profile and people say you're very courageous and all that. But in a way I'm still an eight-year-old girl waiting for her daddy to come home.'

Nora and Breda Power

Nora Power is one of the Birmingham Six wives whose marriage didn't survive the imprisonment of her husband. Originally from

Cork, she still speaks with a strong Cork accent, and is a cheerful, earthy woman. While we talked she was helping her two-year-old grand-daughter with a puzzle. For her, survival meant ending her relationship with Billy Power. She divorced him last year, after ten years of little contact between them.

'I left Birmingham when he was arrested and came to London with two of the kids. My brother took the other two to Cork. I moved back to Birmingham then and lived there until the trial, and Billy's brother took the kids to Belfast. He was a young single bloke, but he took the kids and used to wash them and everything. Billy's sister Patsy gave up her job to go up to Lancaster for the trial.

'I was rehoused then in London. Breda was eight, Lizzy was seven, Patricia was five and Liam was only three. Billy was moved to the Isle of Wight and you'd have to go there. You'd understand how they felt, and they'd have all their little moans, but we'd have to come out after a visit with the kids and that. . . You'd go and you'd come out upset and you'd be upsetting one another. It wasn't doing me any good and I think it wasn't doing him any good. It was very, very hard. Dragging the four kids around on the visits was unbearable. It used to tire me out and I couldn't afford it. You only got money from the social security once a month.

'But I carried on visiting for four and a half or five years. Then I didn't want to do it any more. After that Patsy, Billy's sister, took the kids to see him. I'd have preferred to take the kids myself, but he didn't want it when I was not going to see him.

'My brother gave up his job and came and lived with me and helped with the children. He was marvellous, but I couldn't ask him for the money for the visits all the time.'

However, she participates in the activities of the Birmingham Six campaign, and late last year was hoping the men would be out for Christmas, a hope that was not realised. 'It's not just what they did to the men. The police sentenced six wives and twenty-seven children when they did all that. When he does come out it will be a relief for me anyway. But I'll be honest with you. I wouldn't live with Billy if he got out now. I couldn't. I've got a different life now.'

Does she think of remarrying? 'You must be joking! Once bitten, twice shy!' Three of her four children live nearby, with only the youngest, Liam, still living at home. The two oldest girls have children of their own, and she enjoys them greatly. 'The house is always packed.'

Yet when the men were released last March she joined in the celebrations with gusto. That night in the Irish Centre in Camden Town, where Billy Power and Paddy Joe Hill were celebrating, she brought the house down with a hearty rendition of *I Still Love You After All These Years*.

Her daughter Breda has emerged as one of the most articulate campaigners on behalf of the men, and one of the sharpest critics of the British police and judicial system. Not only is she a spokeswoman for her father, she is secretary of the London Birmingham Six Committee. She spares the Irish government no more than the British. 'I don't know if I'm English or Irish or what. I don't want to be Irish if that's my government over there. At least the British government looks after its own. If that was six British men held in an Irish jail for something they didn't do they'd be out by now.'

Born in London, where she has lived all her life, she sounds like a Londoner. What sets her apart from young women around her is her anger and passion about the injustice towards, not just her father, but also other victims of miscarriages of justice from different communities in Britain. She has formed a close friendship with the wife of one of the Tottenham Three, convicted, they claim wrongly, of the murder of a policeman during a riot.

She is reluctant to talk about her experience of her father's arrest and imprisonment and its affect on her growing up, feeling she has already given up too much of her privacy to the media in the hope it would help the campaign, only to face the bitter truth that, almost seventeen years later, the men were still in jail. More than almost any other relative of an Irish prisoner, she has had to run the gauntlet of the British and Irish mass media, sometimes hardly recognising the picture of herself and her family they later portrayed.

She spoke to me just after the police case against the

Birmingham Six had finally been abandoned by the British Director of Public Prosecutions, and their release was at last in sight. She was exhausted, just beginning to imagine life without constant campaigning.

'I remember being thirteen or fourteen and writing to Margaret Thatcher about my dad. I got a letter back saying nothing could be done, that it was up to the courts to decide. I decided if the Prime Minister couldn't do anything I couldn't. Then after the first *World in Action* programme a group of people got together to set up a committee. I was eighteen.'

Getting involved in a campaign of public meetings and media interviews was not easy. 'I was always a very modest type of person. I was always the type of person in school if I had to read out something in assembly I'd bunk off. We all had to keep a journal in school and one year I won the prize for the best journal. I had to go up before about 1,000 in assembly to accept the prize, and I took the day off sick and someone had to go up and get it for me.

'But with the campaign I would think this was for my dad, not for me. If it was for myself I couldn't do it. It's all I think about when I do the interviews.

'The first couple of meetings I sat through them and didn't understand a word. The meetings were so boring I nearly fell asleep. I just knew my dad was innocent. I never really went into it. My ideas were very simple. I got thirty copies of Chris Mullin's book and sent them to Prime Ministers and people like that around the world. I learned the hard way that you have to go out and convince people. I went to meetings up and down the country, sometimes speaking to about ten people.

'I would have grown up very naïve. Up until the first *World in Action* programme I did have a very normal life except that I visited a prison. My mum's from Cork and she always protected us. I reckon she's still in a state of shock to this day. I knew nothing when I was eighteen. I didn't even know what the letters 'IRA' stood for. I have to thank her for protecting us.

'My dad's brothers and sisters just think it was a big mistake, that he was in the wrong place at the wrong time. I think that's what it was on the day, but afterwards it was all covered up.

'A lot of people say the first ten years were the hardest, with doors shut in their faces. For the first two or three years of the campaign, doors were shut in our faces, and I had people shouting at me. Now the work load is so great I can't keep up with it.'

Because she came straight into this campaign with no previous political experience, she does not always feel constrained by the formalities of political institutions. 'We went to the CSCE (*Conference for Security and Cooperation in Europe*) conference in Copenhagen last year to lobby delegates. We got there at ten in the morning, and the plane back was at five. I was going mad, thinking we had to meet thirty-five people before we left. Paul May (*the chairman of the campaign*) and Jeremy Corbyn (*British Labour MP*) were filling in forms requesting interviews and all that. I just went into the hall where the conference was going on and found that we were on a balcony and the delegates were only a few feet away from us. I just called over the British delegate and introduced myself and asked if I could speak to him and he came out to talk to us. Then I called the Soviet delegate over, and he came out. We ended up having meetings with twenty-five of the delegates. When we left that evening I felt great.'

But the pressure has extracted a toll on her personal life. 'When I got back to Claire (*her two-and-a half-year old daughter*) I wanted to spend time with her and I couldn't. There was a time she wouldn't come to me, she saw me so little. I felt terrible.

'There have been times when I felt really low. I didn't expect it to end. I used to think — is it ever going to end? I used to think — if not I'm going to be trying to get my dad out of jail for the rest of my life. It became an obsession in the end — you'd got that far you couldn't turn back. I felt I couldn't get on with my own life and ignore it.'

Now that he was about to be released she had started thinking about a different future. She had acquired a lot of skills in dealing with politicians, the media and the law in pursuit of justice for her father. 'I have mixed feelings. I did think I would like a good job working with prisoners. But then I look around the visitors' room in the prison and think I couldn't face it again.

'Do you know what I think would be a real luxury? Having a real holiday once a year, a break from everything, being able to say I'll go away for a weekend with Claire, going to the zoo, maybe going for a swim once a week. And not having to worry, not thinking every time I hear the word Birmingham that it's to do with the six men.

'I've suffered from a lot of stress-related health problems. When the Guildford Four were released I lost my voice for three days. You can't have normal relationships. Danny (*her partner*) and I haven't been out just socially for three years. I couldn't have done it without Danny, yet when his mother died last year I wasn't there for him. I really loved her. She was my dad's cousin, and she was really my best friend. But I haven't been able to grieve for her. In the past five years five people I was close to have died, and I haven't been able to grieve for any of them. When my dad's out I'll probably be crying for months!

'I feel for other people in jail, and I'll help out when I can, but I feel that platform is there for them because of the Birmingham Six and the Guildford Four. If I'm asked to speak about injustice and what happened to my dad and there's no one to do it I will. But it won't be high profile like it was.'

Rose McLaughlin

These notorious cases are not the only instances of Irish people being wrongly imprisoned in Britain. There is the case of Judith Ward, who, though not Irish but English living in Ireland, was convicted of a bombing of which no one who knows her thinks she was capable.

Other cases have also given rise to disquiet among lawyers and those concerned with Irish prisoners. One of them is that of Pat McLaughlin from Derry, who was convicted of conspiracy to cause explosions and sentenced to life imprisonment in 1985. Like Nora Power, his wife found the separation and the visits too much to bear, and the relationship came to an end. Now his mother, Rose, visits him in prison in England.

Pat had gone to England to find work after his youngest child

85

died in a cot death at the age of seven months. Like Gerry Conlon, he stayed in an Irish hostel and hung around with young Irish people, drinking a bit and, according to his family, feeling grief-stricken and bewildered at the death of the baby. Failing to find work, he returned to Derry, where he was arrested.

'He was lifted out of his home and taken to Castlereagh. He was out of here in less than thirty six hours,' said his mother. He was questioned about the bombing of Chelsea barracks and charged with conspiracy to cause explosions. His fingerprints had been found on a bin-liner that was associated with the bombing and his name was written in books found in a van allegedly used. At the trial attention was also drawn to an IRA tattoo on his arm.

He was convicted and sentenced to life imprisonment. Three years later he lost an appeal, although, according to his sister Valerie, there were twenty seven discrepancies in the evidence. 'The judge made mistakes, like calling me his mother-in-law from Belfast,' said his mother. 'He was always writing his name in books and he put that mark on his arm when he was twelve or thirteen. I work as a cleaner in the tech' and all the kids up there, Protestant and Catholic, write "Up the IRA" and "Up the UDA" on walls and things. That's what it's like, growing up in this environment. I gave evidence about that in court, but they took me off the stand very quickly.

'They weren't interested, it's as simple as that. Pat was always with me here in the house. He did decorating with his father. We were devastated when it happened, but who do you turn to? I don't know. Father Ryan in the hostel in Kilburn wrote to TDs in Dublin saying "Is this going to be another innocent man sentenced?"'

Now the family is concentrating on getting Pat transferred to a prison in Northern Ireland, and then fighting the conviction, as they find they cannot do so when he is so far away. Further, Pat himself is demoralised and depressed by what has happened, and the break-up of his marriage has been a further blow. 'He would want to write out protesting his innocence,' said his mother. 'But he's a very quiet fellow. Paul Hill said when he got out that anyone in there who did anything boasted about it, but Pat didn't.' His application for transfer has already been turned down on the grounds that the seriousness of his offence does not make it appropriate for him to be transferred and to benefit from the more generous remission terms in the North.

'I wrote a personal letter to Mr Hurd, explaining his background and all,' Rose said. 'The first person who came to talk to me about Pat was Nuala Kelly from the ICPO in Dublin. They're trying to do something. Bishop Daly wrote to Mr Hurd, but Bishop Daly just shakes his head. He said we were trying for years for Shane Doherty. John Hume has gone to visit him, and I had a few letters from Cardinal O Fiaich, God have mercy on him. I wrote to a lot of people, but after a while you lose heart.'

Meanwhile they are trying to keep in touch with Pat, who is depressed and despairing about his situation, and does not write much. 'We went to see him once a year; it was all we could afford. We treated it as our holiday, though going there was no holiday, believe me. His wife used to try to go every two months. Now we're trying to keep the children in touch and we have to go every few months.'

Rose suffers from high blood pressure, is an asthmatic, and finds the journey very stressful. 'I have to spend a week in my bed when I get back. I get invalidity benefit for my blood pressure, but I'm not entitled to help with the journey because his wife had that. Now I'm trying to be registered to go to see him with the children instead of his wife. I suppose for my sake when I go over he keeps his spirits up. Those older ones over there don't care what they say to the screws, and they look after Pat a bit.'

The experience of the Birmingham Six means that others who think they or their relatives have been victims of a miscarriage of justice have little hope that their cases will be redressed quickly, if at all. Rose says: 'I don't think I'll ever see him out. I pray away for peace, but it seems to be getting worse, catholics and protestants are growing further apart. The only march I'd go on is a peace march; that's what we all want. But now I think all we have to look forward to is a transfer.' The experience of the Conlons in seeking transfers does not augur well for Pat McLaughlin and the seventeen year wait of the Birmingham Six does not give him much hope for a review of his conviction.

The record is not reassuring. Both the Guildford Four and the Birmingham Six have served the equivalent of life sentences already. Judith Ward, who had no family or close friends to lobby for her, is still in prison. More disturbing still, many of the factors at work in the 1970s which led to the discredited convictions remain in place. New police procedures and new rules of evidence make the crude forcing of confessions out of suspects much less likely to occur. However, more subtle manipulation of juries through leaks to the press and the holding of IRA-suspected cases in garrison towns, the use of the hostility of sections of the press towards Irish nationalism, the widespread use of conspiracy charges which are difficult to disprove, and, above all, the continued existence of a prosecution and judicial system unchanged despite the damning revelations of the past two years, makes it likely that more miscarriages of justice against Irish people will occur. It remains to be seen whether the Royal Commission set up after the release of the Birmingham Six will redress these problems.

Chapter Three

Hanging On

All the families of prisoners in Britain who live in Northern Ireland, whether or not they contest the convictions, want the prisoner to be transferred to the North. Their eagerness for this almost makes it seem that imprisonment in the North is pleasant.

Compared with imprisonment in Britain this is so. It is far easier for the families, who can visit as often as once a week, with a long bus journey, at most, to face. The expense, trauma and disruption are drastically reduced. The families are part of a larger group from their area for whom prison visiting is part of a routine. They can share experiences and support each other travelling to and fro on the buses. At the prison, conditions have greatly improved for them in recent years, largely through the efforts of voluntary groups like the Quakers, who provide warm canteens and facilities for children.

For the prisoners too it is much easier. Because the number of prisoners in Northern Ireland who are serving very long sentences on serious charges is disproportionately high, the prison system has been redesigned with them in mind. Because their offences are politically motivated, and the prisoners are almost always part of an organisation when they come in, they remain organised inside, which has a major impact on their morale and on their relationship with the authorities. A woman who has one relative in prison in Britain and a son in Long Kesh described the difference as follows: 'When I go to Long Kesh they're out, they're dressed in their own clothes, they're happy, calling to each other. They look as if they're not in prison. When I went to England they were all so pale, dressed in navy prison clothes. There was a wanting look about them.'

The authorities learned just how emotive the prison issue was during the hunger strikes at the beginning of the eighties which drew a majority of the nationalist community in the North, and a sizeable section of the people of Ireland as a whole, around the prisoners and their demands. It would be counter-productive to reproduce the conditions for the re-emergence of the prisoners as an issue. Fergus Cooper, the press officer for the Northern Ireland Association for the Care and Resettlement of Offenders (NIACRO), explains it as follows: 'There's a higher percentage of life-sentenced prisoners here than in Britain and they need more services. It's in the interests of the government to depoliticise the prisons, so you get a high level of cooperation from it.' According to NIACRO, the prison regime in Northern Ireland is more enlightened than in Britain.

This is reflected in the policies towards life-prisoners and those held 'On the Secretary of State's Pleasure,' whose sentences are reviewed after ten and eight years respectively, with a view to setting a release date and granting home leave. They are prepared for their release by a 'work-out' scheme, where they work in the community and live in the prison. Life-prisoners in Britain sweat out twenty years in jail with no hope of respite. However, the review system has come in for a lot of criticism, as the criteria on which prisoners are given release dates are very vague and are seen as arbitrary, and prisoners may be 'knocked back' for reconsideration two to five years later, causing great stress to them and their families. This has given rise to campaigns in both the loyalist and republican communities for changes in the review system.

Nonetheless, life is still very hard for the families. Loyalists have not attacked targets in Britain (although some with Scottish links have been charged with arms offences there), and so rarely face arrest and conviction in Britain. However, they have attacked targets, usually people they suspect of republican sympathies, in the North, and the prisons of Northern Ireland house some three hundred loyalist prisoners, some of them there since the mid 1970s. Loyalist prisoners and their families do not have the strong networks of support enjoyed by republican prisoners, though, especially in the 1970s, they enjoyed community support. The republican support organisations go back to the Relatives' Action Committees in the late 1970s, later absorbed into the H-Block committees during the hunger strike. While these no longer exist, Sinn Féin has a well-organised department dealing with prisoners, and numerous sub-committees dealing with specific problems like the transfer issue or life-sentenced prisoners. Such organisations are at the embryonic stage on the loyalist side.

One such group is Justice for Lifers, founded on 3 May, 1985 by a group of women, one of whom was Hester Dunne. Its primary objective was to seek changes in the review system. In the past year another group, Justice for All, has been formed. It describes itself as 'a non-political, non-sectarian group that has emerged from the need for a voice within the loyalist community to highlight the injustices that permeate our society'. It is run by a former shop steward in Harland and Wolff, William Smith, who is now applying the skills he learned in that role to community work on the Shankill Road.

'There is no organised grouping in the loyalist community working on this,' he said, 'and there are no records kept. For example, there's no record of the exclusion orders (*under the PTA*) against loyalists, though there's plenty of them about. There is nothing for people to plug into. The legal system is so complicated and so hard to get at, people think it's like something they see in the movies. There's a stigma attached to a prisoner's family right away by the police, the authorities, the NIO and the prison officers. That family's guilty, but the family and the relatives have committed no crime.'

Like Hughes and other commentators, he stressed the difficulties faced by the families. 'The prisoner doesn't have to worry about meals on the table, about bills coming in, about where to get his clothes. His wife is left to carry the can, to worry about schools and clothes for the children, bills, food, etc. If she has a wee lad she's worried about him getting involved with the paramilitaries. As the kids grow up they often don't want to go up to the jail. Luckily in Northern Ireland you still have extended families and mothers and sisters help out. Otherwise the wives would go crazy.'

Hester Dunne agrees. 'Wives and girlfriends going up on the

bus support each other, they have so much in common. You watch them coming up, first with their babies in their arms, then with toddlers, and now with young teenagers. I know men who don't have it in them to do what the women have done. They have the loneliness to cope with. He won't have that. He'll have his peers to help him cope with it, to talk to. If she has a young family she can't go out.'

William Smith went on to describe the conditions under which the prisoners and their families had to cope. 'There's no public transport up to the Maze. There's the paramilitaries' buses or the 'Peace bus', but for that you have to go into town and very few people use it. No consideration is given by the DHSS to the families having a person inside and having to make up parcels with cigarettes, fruit, toiletries, newspapers and all that. One young girl told me it cost her £30 a week to keep her husband inside.'

He is also critical of the prison officers.'There is a high level of unemployment in the loyalist areas and there are a lot of jobs in the security services. The prison officers were used as pawns when they introduced the criminalisation policy and told the officers to treat the prisoners like criminals. Some did it with more vigour than others. With the need for increased recruitment they lowered the standards and lowered the quality of recruits. They were not interested in the prisoners' welfare; they had no intensive training and discipline was poor. There are licensed premises on all the prisons in Northern Ireland (*staff clubs within the security of the prison walls*), and there is an element among the prison officers who come on duty drunk.

'Then there are all these petty regulations, and there's no need for them all. Ninty-five per cent of prisoners who had special category status never went back to jail. Because of the regime there they came out without a chip on their shoulder, because one thing they kept while they were in prison was their dignity. Those who come out now who had no special status are full of resentment and that affects their families too.'

Meanwhile the families, especially the wives, struggle to maintain their relationships with the prisoners and to keep a home for their children. But they all find it difficult, and not all survive. 'There is no research or statistical work on this, but every marriage is put under stress by imprisonment,' said Tony Caffney, the head of the Sinn Féin department dealing with prisoners, himself a former prisoner for fifteen years. 'Most marriages and relationships don't survive long-term imprisonment, but the break-up often comes after release. Those that do survive are very strong and very open.

'The point of sentencing is probably worse for the prisoner. What is he sentencing his wife to? He will often say to his wife or girl-friend,"Take yourself off," though he'll really mean, "Don't let go." It is the partner on the outside who pulls the relationship through that crisis, rather than the prisoner.

'At the point of imprisonment both people have to look at what's in front of them. After about five or six years both people will have changed a lot, and they won't necessarily have changed in every way together. The wives will have been forced to take on all sorts of responsibilities they didn't have before. They see a sort of life they want to keep up. There are even relatives involved in campaign work now who would have said they were very happy just with their home life and now they're sitting down to do interviews with people like you, and they would have refused if their husbands were there. After release the couple have to get to know each other again. There has to be an openness that may not have been there before, to maintain the relationship. There is no shame in someone sitting crying their eyes out on a visit.'

Sometimes the wife may contract another relationship while her husband is in prison. This in turn can lead to difficulties. There is a tradition in the republican movement that wives and girlfriends are expected to be loyal and faithful to their jailed partners, and they have been assisted in this by vigilance on the part of the movement outside, which has been known to warn off potential suitors. On the loyalist side too there have been instances of the prisoner's associates or family leaning on the woman to discourage her from associating with other men.

This is changing, according to Tony Caffney: 'Prisoners' wives and girlfriends were expected to be paragons of chastity. In clubs and that there was the practice where people would check if the woman they fancied was a prisoner's wife or girlfriend. There was also a time when a prisoner would send out word if he heard that someone was going out with his wife or girlfriend, and tell the movement to do something about it.

'That's changing now, and there's more the attitude that if she has a fling they don't want to know. Men are starting to think: "If I was outside and she was inside, would I remain faithful?" Most men wouldn't. Ironically it has got to the stage where the prisoner can accept something like that better than the community. This community is very incestuous. Everyone knows everyone, and it can turn on someone and be very vicious.'

A social worker who worked in the Visitors' Centres in Long Kesh and Maghaberry added that women left alone felt vulnerable to harassment and stayed near their parents or in-laws for protection. 'There are different stages in the imprisonment for the family. It's like a bereavement. At first there's a period of mourning, then the question of acceptance arises and if they do they build up support systems, etc. After five, six or seven years questions arise again. Then they are maintained by a sense of duty and a routine, the man is not really a part of their life, he is not needed in the same way. The woman is independent, perhaps she is working.

'Some break up at that stage. If they don't then they face a new crisis when the review comes up after ten years to set a release date. The criteria are very vague, so they don't know what is required. They take on the guilt if the prisoner doesn't get a release date. The family feel they did something wrong.

'The loyalists estimate about forty per cent of marriages break down. The majority break down after the release where the men return to their old ways.'

Yet most prisoners' wives struggle to maintain the relationship, even in the face of very long sentences of twenty and more years. In doing so both they and their relationships change.

Dolores

Dolores's husband Phil is serving his second sentence for IRA activity. Four years ago he was sentenced to sixteen years for possession of explosives, of which he expects to serve eight. He previously served six and a half years of a ten-year sentence.

'We were married when he was going on eighteen; he had to get permission from his mother. We spent the first few years in Buncrana where he was on the run, then he was arrested. Sinéad was two and a half when he was sentenced for the first time. He was out for two and half years after that and she was just going into the big school and I was pregnant with Gráinne when he was arrested the second time. Out of seventeen years of married life we've spent six and a half years together.'

His second arrest put a strain on their relationship. 'I was always arguing with him about it. He knew what he was doing. Then he goes and throws it all away by getting lifted again with a baby coming. I was angry. He shouldn't have been in that flat when it was raided. There was an argument there and he went out in a huff, and at five o'clock in the morning the police came here. The raid was so bad here I thought he'd got away. After he got lifted the first time I'd said, "If you're ever lifted again I'll never visit you again. It's all over." I went up with his sister to see him. I thought I'd kill him. Then I saw him and he was all beat up. He said, "I'm sorry," and I said, "It's OK, I'll be up to visit you."

'When I walked into the empty house after that visit my sisters were there, Sinéad was there, but I felt I was alone. I felt like bursting out crying. Maybe it was just as well I was pregnant. It made me look after myself.

'Your whole lifestyle changes. The first time he was inside I was up to see him every week. Now we're both more mature, I go up every fortnight on the bus Sinn Féin lays on. It costs £3.50, and another £3.50 for Sinéad, though she's still in school. I get up about 6.30 in the morning on the days I go to visit and get Gráinne in a good mood before bringing her to her granny. I bring her up about once a month. On the other visits I come back with crisps or sweets or a book and I always say, "Look what your daddy sent you out."

'I don't know what's going to happen to us next week or the week after. I've gone up on the bus with more friends of mine, and their marriages split up, split up through jail. We were only together for two years before he was jailed this time. But there's people married a whole lifetime who don't have what we had. He was a husband and friend all rolled into one. That's why I keep going up.

'At the beginning if he asked me would I wait for him I said, "Aye." Now we can talk about it. We got closer through writing letters.

'The loneliness is the worst, sitting in at night. I have Sinéad, and we get on the best. But it's not the same. I have to take all the decisions myself and go to the school about Sinéad. The first time I had a job in the Bogside Inn, but now I can't afford to get anyone to look after Gráinne. I'm fed up not having a few pennies.

'I write twice a week, but you don't like putting everything in a letter because they read it. There's a friend of mine was living with a fellow who was lifted the same time as Phil. She met someone else and they split up. The screws did their best to taunt him about it. He pays no attention. He's an old hand. But I wouldn't write personal things or things happening in the family in a letter. You can smuggle in letters sometimes and put your feelings in. You do get your down days. He knows by my letters, though I thought my letters were OK. But he can read between the lines.'

Although she leads a very quiet life, she feels pressure from the community to present a decorous front. 'I go out every Tuesday night to a bar with these friends of mine, a couple. It's full of old-age pensioners. One of them asked me if my friend was "your brother". I knew what was going through her mind. I saw prisoners' wives out before and dancing or talking with someone and you'd see all the heads turning. People in Derry take prisoners' wives too much for granted. They expect too much. You're allowed a few drinks, but not to get tipsy and not to dance.

'A friend of mine met someone else. Thank God it never happened to me, but I can't say what'll happen next week. I've said, "I'll do my best."

'I know about five marriages of prisoners who split up over the years, people coming up on the bus I'd only know to see. There would be people having affairs as well, but that's always blown out of proportion. The fellows must talk about it. One girl I know, her husband was on the blanket (*the protest which preceded the hunger strikes*) and she has a baby. The fellow got out later and they're together and as happy as anything. He got into religion and I think that helped him accept it.'

Like many prisoners and their families, Dolores is not religious herself. 'The priests get up my nose. I go to mass sometimes, but I blame the priests for half the bother. The bishop here told people to tell their local police what was going on in their areas. Elderly people did that, thinking they were doing right by the Catholic Church, and faced being shot as informers. I blame the priests.'

Although she is angry with her husband for getting arrested again and leaving her alone, she sympathises with his views. 'One of his mates was blown up and I think, maybe it's as well he's inside. He could be up in the cemetery. I'm behind them all the way. I wasn't at the beginning, but as the years go on you get deeper into it. Don't get me wrong. If he was here now and he was going out, I'd say, "Are you going out to play cowboys and Indians?" I wouldn't mind him being involved in Sinn Féin. I just don't want him getting involved (*in the IRA*) again. If he goes inside again, I'll kill him. It'll be me doing time and not him. But if he did I'd have to accept it. It'd be that or split up. Knowing me I'd just take it as it comes.

'I'll stick up for them though a lot of families turn against them. When it started off way back in the 1970s we said, "It'll only last a few months." It was the same with the blanket protest and the hunger strikes, we thought they would only last a few months, and ten had to die. I wish it was all over.'

Marilyn

Marilyn is the wife of a loyalist prisoner, Dennis, who has served four years of an eleven-year sentence. They have three sons aged between eight and twelve, the eldest of whom is now living with his grandparents.

Marilyn, a woman in her thirties, with short blonde hair and sad blue eyes, has had more than the average share of troubles. 'It was a very big shock when he was arrested. I'm Scottish myself, I never knew what trouble was until I came here. I know Dennis worries about us too, but at the end of the day it's the wife who has everything to carry on her shoulders, trying to clothe the kids, make ends meet, keep the house decent. I have good in-laws, otherwise I'd never have coped.'

'My parents died after I came over here, and then my brother. My world just fell apart. Then when Dennis went to prison it was a worse loss. My world will still be apart until he comes out and we can be a family again. When I go out in the summer and see families doing things together it hurts.

'The social security treat me as a single parent, yet I have to bring in parcels. The children get their dinner in school some days. Then they can have scrambled eggs in the evenings. I always make sure they get a good dinner on Sunday.

'When he first went in I started drinking thinking it would help me sleep. It didn't. It just added to the problems. I tried to kill myself a year after he went in, with the guilt of the drinking and feeling I was doing wrong for him and the kids. I took an overdose. But from that day I never looked back. It had to be me that made the decision. I wanted to be there for the kids. I started to pull myself up.'

Then another disaster struck. Her middle child, also called Dennis, was affected worse than the other two by the imprisonment and was already showing signs of being disturbed. Some three years into his father's sentence he was taken up the glen and sexually abused by an older boy who was charged and then allowed out on bail, so he was still in the neighbourhood. Dennis's school work started to deteriorate and his behaviour became very aggressive. 'Do you know what he's playing now? Jails! That's all he does day in, day out. He sees his Daddy once a month, but the visits are a bit disruptive. He wants his Daddy all to himself. Then Darren (*the younger child*) sees Dennis getting away with so much after what happened to him so he acts up, which is an extra strain. Sometimes you go to bed at night and hope you wake up and everything will just be all right.'

Dennis is now going to a special centre for children with problems three mornings a week, and Marilyn attends counselling there twice a week. 'I'm the only protestant there with a lot of catholics. There's no religion in it, just women with problems with their kids. Before I started going up there I had nobody.

'There's great hostility from the neighbours. They're always coming to the door complaining about Dennis, and sending the police to the door. He goes to the ordinary school two days a week, and sometimes they send him home. He's a troubled wee boy, definitely. I'm afraid he'll be taken off me into care. That's my big fear.'

She does not get support from the local community, or from any political network linked to the organisation of which her husband was a member when he went to jail. She rents a house in a private estate in North Belfast. 'I haven't very good neighbours. The people here look down on you because you've got someone in prison, and they also look down on you because you're a woman bringing up children alone.

'It's lonely, like, but it's something you get used to. There's times I went to bed and cried and wondered why this ever happened to us. I never go out. I go to bed when the kids go to bed, just to get peace. Now they expect me to go to bed when they do. Every night I write ten pages to him. I've done it for four years.

'I was out with Prisonlink (*a self-help group for prisoners' relatives*) last Tuesday night. It was the first time I was out in I don't know how long. I often thought of going back to Scotland, but my love for him is too strong. Not only that, the kids love their father, and I wouldn't put them through that. I've told him, though, if he gets into trouble when he's out I'll leave him.

'It's going to be hard when he gets home, hard for both of us. I've got my independence, which I never had. The dinner was always on the table, and all that. Now I seem to be stronger than I ever was.' Does her husband expect things to be the way they were before when he gets out? She gave a rare, wry smile. 'He

99

knows the score.

'Before he went to prison whenever we had a row we never talked it through. I'd get angry and it'd end in a big fight. We talk now. All we do is talk. It's all we can do. I visit once a week. You get one and a half hours in Long Kesh, in cubicles. There's more privacy there and the kids can sit on his knee and that.'

Marilyn is angry at a system she sees as punishing the families who have done nothing. 'The women do the bigger sentence. It's as if they're guilty too. When the judge passes the sentence he should take that into consideration. He can say, when his wife stands in the court, "I'm sentencing you too."

'The husband has done wrong, and should pay for what he did wrong. But this way they're sentencing the whole family. I don't think taking a man away from his family does any good. If he had to go somewhere every day, do hard labour someplace, and sign on in the police barracks and be in at a certain time, he would still be there to take some of the pressure off the wife.

'If the husbands knew what strain they put on their wives and children I don't think half of them would do what they do. It all brought home to him how important his family is. All he ever talks about is getting home and moving out and starting a new life.'

Patricia

There are some women who marry prisoners in prison, in the full knowledge of what they have to face. According to Hughes, many of these marriages are strong and supportive. He had reservations, however: 'When two people are married in prison, having formed their relationship since the imprisonment began, they can enjoy no privacy or time together from the time of their marriage onwards. It is not unreasonable to deduce, therefore, that the marriage will be prevented from consummation. In such cases, the very legality of the marriage must be suspect. Therein lies a difficulty, often raised by the author, but as yet no satisfactory answer has been forthcoming. It illustrates official insensitivity towards the needs of marriage.'

Patricia and Adrian, both from Derry, were going out for

about a year when he was arrested and sentenced to life imprisonment for killing a policeman. She was twenty, he a couple of years older. She is now twenty eight, small and pretty, fashionably dressed, with blonde, high-lighted hair. No one seeing her in the street or in a pub could guess at her circumstances. 'I was not prepared for him going to jail right up to the day of the trial. Then I carried on visiting, and we got engaged the Valentine's Day after he was sentenced.' She is rather reticent, but it is clear that she fought for the relationship against the opposition of both sets of parents and even of Adrian himself. 'Our mothers wanted us to call it off. They had me tortured, saying, "You should live your own life."'

Adrian also wanted to give Patricia the opportunity to live her own life, so the engagement was broken off. 'I didn't want to go out with anyone else. You're always sure of what you want. After six months I decided that he was it and he started to arrange for the wedding. We waited for seven and a half years.

'The day of the wedding they took us through the search and everything. They took the money my father had for the priest off him. We queued up and went through the turnstile, carrying the wedding cake. I was nervous on the way up, but with all the hassle I got angry.

'The wedding ceremony was lovely. There were three priests, the prison chaplain, a monk and a cousin. Adrian's best man was someone from inside close to him. It would have been one of his brothers if he was out, but in there you have to have someone from inside, so that there was someone there for him when we all left. Then we had tea, sandwiches and cake, all in the chapel. Normally you get an hour visit after, but we didn't. I went up to visit him the next day.'

'There were eleven of us. It was lovely, very intimate,' added her mother-in-law, Lily. 'The screws were singing and all. But it was very sad when we came to go. It was a marriage in name only.'

In four more years' time Patricia can hope that Adrian will get out on home leave, but until then they won't have spent a moment alone together since their marriage or throughout their long engagement. If he serves his full sentence Patricia will be forty when Adrian is released, and it may be too late to have a family. 'I would really, really love to have a family, but if it can't be it can't be. Adrian loves children, but it's not our own choice. There's enough in our families anyway, I have six sisters and three brothers.

'Brian (*her father-in-law*) is saying we should fight for conjugal visits and all that, but I don't know if I could accept it. I'd be really embarrassed. If I got pregnant how could I convince people I got pregnant in jail?'

Paradoxically, the imprisonment has brought her and Adrian closer. 'When he was out we just battered on, we never showed how we felt. Then when he went inside he just opened up. He said that's how it is in there.'

However, the long separation is difficult. 'I had a sister who got married last week and I couldn't go. I couldn't take it. They read out a card from Adrian and it would have broken me up. What really choked me up recently was when he asked what was a 20p coin like.'

She goes out on Friday nights with friends, and with Adrian's parents sometimes. This summer she's going on holiday with them to Gweedore, but will still keep up her weekly visits over to Long Kesh. She is looking for a flat, 'but I don't like doing things without him.' Unlike the wives who were already married and mothers when their husbands went in, she does not have the responsibility of a family to look after. But neither does she have the company and comfort of children, or the bond they can form between a couple. She is in a kind of limbo and, unless there is a change in the political situation, will remain there for another twelve years.

Cathleen

Wives who decide to end their relationship with a husband in prison are less visible and less vocal than those who hang on. They often make new lives away from their husband's old friends and family, sometimes with a new partner. If they do they no longer fit into the welfare systems run either by the political organisations to which their husband was linked or by independent or charitable organisations, though some of the latter do try to keep in touch with them.

Yet they too have problems. Their relationship with their first partner may not be fully resolved, and if they have children the prisoner will want to maintain his relationship with them, even if his relationship with their mother is over. If she has another partner he may be unhappy about her maintaining contact with the husband.

Cathleen originally comes from Finglas in Dublin and married Pat when she was seventeen. They had five children in as many years, one of whom died. She was twenty-three when he was arrested in 1985. She visited her husband in prison in England for five years after his arrest but eventually it all became too much for her, and she stopped visiting and formed another relationship. 'I'll still support him any way I can,' she said. 'He's still my husband. I still care about him a lot.

'The visits were terrible. I went once on the boat with the kids and I was ready for a nervous breakdown when I got back. Then I had to get a doctor's letter to get the money for the plane from the brew. They ask you, 'Are you sure you're taking the kids over?' You go down with the doctor's letter to the brew, then to the travel agent, then arrange transport to Belfast to get the plane. I always took two children, and the four at Christmas. The kids would be crying.

'The last few visits were not very good. Every year I was bringing some bad news; there were deaths in the family or something. God knows how he feels.' The relationship was not very strong anyway. 'We were only seventeen when we married. He didn't understand me, I had a kid every year. I had five kids when I was twenty two. He said to the kids once, "I don't know why I got married but I grew to love your mother."

'It was my thirtieth birthday last year, and I didn't even get a card. The kids never got birthday cards, and it means so much to the kids. Things like that got me down. The wains were always upset around the visits. They didn't know whether they were coming or going. They'd be over in their granny's; they were always over and back. And all for what? To be depressed when you got back? With all the hassle, even if we had a good

103

relationship I don't think I could have held out. I'd been on my own so long. You need a friend, you need someone to talk to. The kids were still being punished. They had no daddy to turn to and I had no one to help me with the kids.'

Then Cathleen formed another relationship and got pregnant. 'I was only six stone last Christmas, I lost that much weight with the worry. I was five months pregnant. I was embarrassed all the time. People would be looking at the bump and saying, "poor Pat, poor Pat." But saying that, there's hardly anyone on the street didn't buy that child something when she was born. I was going to give her away, you know.' She turned to the six-month old baby asleep in the living room. 'I wouldn't swap you for the world. Even if I was split up she was the best thing ever happened.'

She told Pat, and he was prepared to accept the baby. 'He said, "After all I did to you, it's the least I can do."' But by now her relationship with the baby's father was steady, and she told him that, though she is not sure what will happen in the future. 'I just want to be friends with Pat, be able to write to him and visit him as a friend, but Liam (*her boyfriend*) won't hear of it.

'I don't know what's around the corner for me, if this is a long-term relationship for me. My head's going round and round. I don't know where I am. Sometimes I feel I can't go on, that I'll do myself in; but you get the strength from somewhere. I don't know what's going to happen in the future. I get tired about everything sometimes. All I wanted was a good family and to love my kids and be happy.

'I feel I've achieved nothing with my life. I've reared kids, kept a home and been a skivvy. That's what my life was about and at the end of the day I hope I'll be appreciated. I wasn't bright. I wanted them to be brighter than me, to do things. I hope to God they don't follow my footsteps. I put them off marriage. I say, "Don't waste your lives". I would dread it if Ciara (*her eldest*) came in and said she was pregnant. I'll never want her to get married even if that happens. She should live with the guy and see what she wants.

'That baby feels like mine. I don't remember having the rest of them, I don't remember being pregnant. Now Ciara is more help with that baby than he was with them.'

She would go home to Dublin, but has no one to go to there. 'Derry's not like Dublin, it's a small community. If anything happened they would help you, but they would backstab you at the same time. You can do nothing in Derry. My own childhood wasn't very happy. My parents wouldn't talk to us. I didn't know what Christmas was; there were no presents or anything. There was always fighting and that.

'In Derry they all have their mothers and their mothers are good to them. Now when Ciara comes in we talk. I can go up the town with my daughter. I have that. I have nobody but my kids. No matter what happens I have them. They're good kids, they can come in and make cups of tea and that. I hope I'll always be there for my children and I'll be able to give things to my grandchildren.' She still has a good relationship with her in-laws. 'Pat's family was the only family I had. My mother-in-law has had so much trouble in her life. They're good people. What did she do that everything went wrong?' Her mother-in-law now brings the children to see their father. 'They're his kids and no one will ever take that away.'

She has no interest in politics, but like most people in Derry has been affected by the political situation. 'There's not one person around here hasn't been affected by the 'troubles,' not one family hasn't been hurt. I'd like to see an end to it, but I don't see it.'

Ending the routine of visits to her husband and starting a new relationship has not solved the problems that arose out of his imprisonment. She still has to cope as a single parent as far as her four eldest children are concerned. She is still concerned about her husband who has always denied any involvement with the offence for which he was convicted. She needs to keep him in touch with his children and she faces an uncertain future in her new relationship. 'You got me on one of my good days. Some days I just cry all day.'

Chapter Four

Spreading the Web

When a person is jailed for a long time the main victims are the wife and children, if they are married. But other members of the family also suffer, and may not even be able to plug into the kind of support system available to the prisoner's dependants. If they are parents they may have been quite unaware of the views and activities of their sons (and daughters, occasionally) and have to cope with the shock of the imprisonment as well as the separation. This is more likely to be the case with loyalist prisoners, as there is no tradition of opposition to the state in the loyalist community, unlike the republican community. Their parents, therefore, are often bewildered as well as upset by the news of their son's involvement.

They have no Relatives' Action Committee, no network of social and fund-raising activities for the families, no political organisation committed to prisoners. Some do break out of their isolation and contact people with similar problems, forming support groups. Others make contact with prisoners' welfare organisations like the Northern Ireland Association for the Care and Resettlement of Offenders (NIACRO). Until recently this organisation was viewed with suspicion by the republican movement, and women linked to republican prisoners tended to avoid it. However, this is changing, and the organisation now cooperates with republican prisoners' organisations on certain issues like the transfer of prisoners in jail in Britain, and provides a space for the discussion of common problems among prisoners' families from both communities.

For some prisoners the effect of their imprisonment on their parents upsets them so much that it shakes their political beliefs and leads them to renounce their convictions. They 'do their time' patiently, waiting only for it to end so that they can re-enter the intimate world of the family they feel they have damaged. For others the experience of imprisonment binds their family into the political community of which they are a part, extending the influence of that community beyond the generation which forms the bulk of the prisoners. Some find other outlets for their passions, and in the case of loyalist prisoners this is often religion.

Gertie

Gertie's son left school at seventeen in 1975. The following November he was arrested and given an indeterminate sentence for murder 'On the Secretary of State's Pleasure,' due to his youth. 'The family was never involved with anyone in prison. It wrecked our lives,' she told a conference of NIACRO. 'For five years we never celebrated Christmas, we never went on holidays. We couldn't celebrate. We felt guilty with our young son in prison.

'We could not talk to our own family and relations. It was as if I was on another planet. One friend of mine said to me, "If I were you and that happened to me I'd commit suicide." I needed someone who came through the same experience.

'I had met other mothers visiting sons with life sentences and on SOSP. I set about contacting them. Each of them wanted someone to talk to. Some of the women could not even talk to their husbands. I decided the group would be a mothers' group, a women's group. In 1984 I contacted a TV producer who made contact with NIACRO. We set up a group of about twelve mothers in Portadown.

'We can talk to each other, which we can't to family and friends. We've met every Tuesday now for seven years. I've known mothers come into us who are drugged because they have to face their sons serving long sentences.' Her own son was released after thirteen years, but she continues her work with the group, which is independent of the state and statutory agencies. Probation officers may come to talk to them, but only if they are invited by the group, while there are other groups which are run jointly by NIACRO and the probation service.

Jean

Jean works with NIACRO, and this is as a direct result of her experience. She is the mother of a son sentenced to life imprisonment for murder in 1979, who was released in 1989. Like Gertie, she was deeply shocked when she learned of his involvement.

'He was twenty when he was convicted, and seventeen when the offence was committed. His father was killed by a bomb when he was thirteen, and that affected him. He got involved in the UVF, but he was out of the organisation for a few years when he was arrested and he thought it was all behind him. Then he was arrested and convicted. He served almost ten years, mainly in Crumlin Road.

'I found it hard to face. I was totally opposed to what he did. I felt we had the army and police to deal with the things he was complaining about. I talked to him about it and I felt more able to face it when he told me he didn't pull the trigger.'

Her son's attitude to his sentence was 'to keep his head down and get on with it'. He had already broken with the organisation before his arrest, and did not want to be part of it inside. But it was not that easy to sever all contact. 'Once he was out the attitude from his old associates was that he was a hero. He rejects that, "I was an eejit. I wasted ten years of my life and turned my mother's hair grey."

'Some do return as heroes, John Wayne and Clint Eastwood rolled into one. They're heroes in the eyes of young men in the area. What happens largely depends on what they have to go back to. Those with few prospects and poor relationships return to a "hard man" status in their areas, especially in the more deprived areas.'

Jean is now working with NIACRO in its centre in Crumlin Road prison, where she meets many prisoners, both republican and loyalist, and their families. Her experience is that the loyalist prisoners tend to get involved very young, between sixteen and twenty. 'Many return to family life when they get out of prison. They do not remain in political activity linked to the organisation they were part of, unlike the republicans. The republicans are pmore likely to be older when they get involved, to stay involved and to return to political activity when they get out.'

James and Eve

James and Eve live in a neat house in what is now a loyalist estate in North Belfast. In the 1960s it was a mixed estate, but when the troubles began the catholics were driven out, as estates were homogenised according to religion all over Belfast. He keeps racing pigeons, and produces letters from correspondents in the south who have received his birds. One of his sons breeds Rottweiler dogs, and the walls are covered with certificates and prizes. He points out those from the Irish Kennel Club. With typical Northern hospitality, tea and homemade scones must be consumed before any talking is done.

Their other son, Jim, is serving a life sentence for murder in Maghaberry prison. He was a fitter in the shipyard and had been married for ten months when he was arrested. He was twenty-three and his wife was twenty-two . 'They had a lovely home,' said Eve. 'She stuck with him for seven years. She used to teach in Sunday school and that. Then Jim was not in jail very long when the house was broken into, and the following winter the house was flooded. She felt God was not there when she needed him and she gave it up.'

They are baffled by what happened to their son. There was no tradition of political activity in the family. 'I was in the British army for six years during the war. He was raised here in a mixed community; you couldn't have got better people. He stood at the door and cried when they moved out,' said James. 'Jim was always brought up to go to Sunday school and Bible class,' said his mother. 'He was in the Boys' Brigade and all that. You do your best and then you wonder where you went wrong.'

Before his arrest the house was searched a few times, and he was taken to Castlereagh interrogation centre. But he always came home. 'The morning he was arrested James had gone to work. I gave them Jim's new address and they arrested him there. It gives you an awful feeling when they come in the middle of the night.'

He was held for fifteen months on remand in Crumlin Road. 'It's very degrading going there,' she continued. 'When you went to see him you had to stand out in the street and people were passing by looking at you. Then he went to the Maze, or Long

Kesh, as they call it. He was in the H-Blocks. He had one visit a week and his wife had most of them. It was just half an hour. It took you so long going there for just one half hour.

'He broke with the organisation about five years after. He told us to take no money or anything. He had a religious conversion about seven years ago and that helps. He got a review after ten years and was put back for five years. His next review will be in a year or so. He's studying maths and English now. He's getting into computers.'

Since his religious conversion he has made contact with co-thinkers elsewhere in Northern Ireland, and they write to him and visit him. 'He has different visitors every week. Our son here goes up to see him and our two daughters. We saw very little of him for the first six years. His wife took all the visits. Now we go up about twice a month. It's a good job we don't smoke or drink! He asked us if it was OK to put in for Maghaberry (*the conforming prison*), because it was a bit further for us. We said to do what was best for him. In the other place they call the prison warders screws and that and I don't like that.'

The visits have kept them close. 'We don't write, though we send cards and that. He wrote once when he first went in and apologised for all the trouble and all.' What was the biggest hardship? 'It was only not having him. His room's still up there, waiting for him.'

Like many life-sentenced prisoners he got home leave in the summer. 'He cried from the time we lifted him till we got him here. He thought the house was very small after the prison. His sister flew home from New Zealand to see him. It was the first time the family was together for fourteen years.' Photographs of the family reunion are produced. 'He'll be out for Christmas again. There'll be no worry about his parcel this Christmas. We had to break up all the chocolate before because Semtex can be made to look like chocolate, and we had to slice the turkey, the meat and the Christmas cake and put the shortbread in clear covering in case there was something hidden in them.'

They are hoping his release date will be set soon, and that he can come out and resume a normal life. According to his parents, Jim has put his political involvements behind him and now wants to practise his religious convictions and work with children. 'All he talks about now is the neighbours, sport, what programmes we watch on TV. He doesn't talk about what is happening inside.'

How do they see the future? 'Gabriel and the archangels couldn't bring peace to this country. The ones sitting at the top don't want to lose their money,' said James. 'When you look at other countries you see starving and all, and no one goes short here. You wonder what they're fighting for,' said Eve.

Margaret

James and Eve feel bewildered by what has happened to disrupt their quiet, law-abiding, religious lives. Their neighbour, Margaret, is also bewildered, but she is angry as well, though she is not sure where to direct her anger. Both her father and brother are life-sentenced prisoners. She is married with her own family, but she visits her father and brother faithfully.

'They're in their fourteenth year. They were all arrested within weeks of each other and charged. My parents are separated for five or six years now as a result of jail. If it wasn't for the troubles here the jails would be empty.'

Her father and brother are in separate prisons so on the day of the visit she gets up early and gets the children off to school before setting out, first to Long Kesh, then to Maghaberry. 'I get to Long Kesh about ten. If there's a strike on you can wait for two or two and a half hours before being called. You get a good long visit in Maghaberry in a big room. An orderly comes and takes orders for tea and biscuits and the Quakers run the canteen there for the families, which is good. The staff in Maghaberry treat you better.'

Her father is fifty-five. 'He'll be getting the old-age pension when he comes out. Robert had his bowel removed and has a bag now. Now Daddy is bleeding from the back and I wasn't contacted, and I'm the next of kin since my parents separated. He's still the boss in the family. I bring the children up to see him and he tells them to go to school and that. My eldest is twelve. She's been going since she was two weeks old. That's what my daddy missed out on. All the lifers want is to come out and sit by the fireside with their families.'

Like Jim, her father got out on home leave over the summer. 'I had the house gleaming. I went to bed the night before and I couldn't go to sleep with my nerves. When Daddy came out he didn't even notice what was on the floor. I felt very unsettled after he went back. I wasn't myself for a few months. They'll both be out for Christmas now. There'll be a big family reunion. He'll be home for my birthday. The last time was when I was eighteen. The way I look at it, now there's a light at the end of the tunnel. At least they'll come home.'

Like many prisoners, her brother has done a degree in prison. 'He's got a BA already, and he's going to do honours. He was offered a place in a Canadian university when he gets out, but the Canadian government won't allow it. He hopes to go to Oxford or Cambridge.' Because of the colostomy, they tried to get him early release on health ground, 'but no way. The Price sisters got out on health grounds with anorexia,' she adds bitterly.

Like her neighbours, she feels that the troubles are the result of someone, somewhere, doing well out of it, and spreads her scorn around among the founders of the civil rights movement and the leaders of the armed organisations now active. 'It's all socialists behind it, behind the civil rights and that, and communists. In the 1970s those involved (*on the loyalist side*) thought they were doing it for a cause. There's no cause now. This generation is a big mafia. You see these ones living on the brew and they go off to Spain on their holidays. You get businessmen in suits running it all. They're probably all from England, Scotland, Australia.'

Lily and Brian

Lily and Brian are the parents of Adrian, the republican prisoner from Derry who received a life sentence for having driven a vehicle involved in the shooting of a policeman. (Adrian married Patricia, who was interviewed above). Lily is also the sister of John Walker of the Birmingham Six. She is a warm, hospitable woman, and the family live in an old, comfortable house near the city centre. The bond between Adrian and his parents has brought them closer to the republican movement.

'My family wasn't republican at all until these troubles, although Brian's was,' said Lily. 'I remember sitting in The Diamond in the city centre singing *We Shall Not Be Moved* and saying to Brian, 'This is for our families.' If I thought then that I'd be round the prisons of England to see John and up to Long Kesh to visit Adrian I think I'd have killed myself.'

Brian produced photographs of Adrian who was a champion schoolboy swimmer, and cuttings reporting his triumphs, including his swim of the channel. There are photos of his other sons as well, also swimmers. 'That's what I reared my sons for,' he said sadly, 'to be locked up.'

'When Adrian was inside for a few months, Brian got laid off,' continued Lily. 'We were sending up three parcels a week. It was costing £37 a week. We were going to sell the house. But you always manage, you get there.'

His arrest was a shock, but not really a surprise. 'Being his mother and us being very close, I knew he was involved. If he was out at night I never slept until he came in. Rearing a family here is very hard. At first I could not understand how my son, with how he was brought up, his swimming and all, would want to lay down his life. He explained it to me, how he felt and his beliefs, and I thought if I was young maybe I would do the same. I do believe in fighting for your rights.

'I wouldn't like him to get involved in order to be a big man or anything like that, but I would like him to fight for what he believes in. Your heart is pounding out of your body when they say they're involved, but you have to respect their rights to what they believe in.

'I took a mild stroke the night he was lifted. It nearly killed me. I paced the floor the whole night before the trial, but that day in court I said to him, "Hold your head up high and be proud, son, because I'm proud of you." And he held his head up. Adrian said it must be terrible for John (*Walker, his uncle*) to be in prison and not be involved in anything, "At least I was involved," he said.'

Lily and Brian and their children visit Adrian regularly, and they're clearly a close-knit family. They tried to dissuade Patricia from committing herself to marrying him ('It was a life sentence for her too,' explained Brian) but now that she has they are glad. 'I always think that with Patricia there if something happened to Brian and me there's someone there for him,' said Lily.

Like their counterparts on the loyalist side, they do not see a quick end to the troubles in the North. 'He'll serve his time like the rest of the men. It's gone on too long now to turn back. I don't see a solution, not in the near future anyway.'

Mary Cullen

Mary Cullen's son Finbar, with Martina Shanahan and John McCann, was jailed for twenty-five years for conspiracy to murder in 1988, but acquitted on appeal eighteen months later. She differs from the majority of parents of Irish prisoners in being a professional woman from the South, to whom the troubles in the North were fairly distant until the arrest of her son. She and the families of the other two are also exceptional in that they quickly generated a campaign in support of the three, and they won their case on appeal. The whole experience has profoundly influenced her attitude to questions of law, justice, and thinking in the south on the situation in the North.

The three families came together within a few weeks of the arrests and met the Irish Commission for Prisoners Overseas, with which she already had contact. They set up a support group with the help of the ICPO, started to raise public awareness of the facts of the case, contacted politicians and sought Irish government observers at the trial and an expression of concern from it to the British authorities about the charges, the evidence and the location and timing of the trial.

An ad-hoc all party Oireachtas committee with over thirty public representatives was set up. 'It was the first time such an ad-hoc committee had been set up so quickly,' said Mary Cullen. 'It happened in the atmosphere generated by the Birmingham Six and Guildford Four case and it is a very encouraging development for other cases and campaigns.'

This continued after the conviction, which was controversial for a number of reasons, in particular because of the intervention of Tom King, the former Northern Ireland Secretary and the alleged victim of the conspiracy. Towards the end of the trial, on the day it was reported that the three had decided to exercise their right to silence, he held a press conference as Home Secretary at which he announced the British government's decision to abolish the right to silence and said that IRA suspects regularly used the right to silence to avoid conviction. His intervention and its likely effect on the jury was the ground on which the appeal was later successful.

After the convictions the three families continued the regular trek to England to visit. Martina's sister Deirdre had already fallen victim to one of the dangers facing Irish families visiting relatives in Britain when she was excluded from Britain under the Prevention of Terrorism Act, and would be unable to see her sister until after her release. However, Mary Cullen herself escaped many of the problems experienced by other families visiting prisons. She wonders if her middle class status was a factor in this. 'The prison officers were very polite on the whole.' she said. 'I found the security at the airports more stressful. You never knew what their reaction would be when you told them who you were going to see. Some of them were very stiff, almost hostile, when you told them.'

After talking to Finbar she sees prisoners in a different light. 'You came to realise that every prisoner was a person with her or his own life and problems, and with their individual anxieties about their futures, their health, their families. You also began to wonder about the whole role of prisons in society, and what purposes they serve. You learned the importance of regular family visits to maintain relationships, and the financial pressure on many families to keep up visits to England. I have a reasonable salary and yet I felt the pressure, so what must it be like for people living on social welfare? This whole area of prisoners and their families is one we all need to be concerned about.'

But it was in her perception of the justice system that her assumptions were shaken most deeply. 'Even though I had read Chris Mullin's book and believed the Birmingham Six were innocent I still assumed that when people were arrested and charged they were usually guilty, and that the police knew they were. Now when I read about anyone being arrested anywhere I wonder.

'I learned a lot about miscarriages of justice and how what happens in a courtroom is influenced by what happens outside it. In our case, at the start we saw a lot of separate bits that were obviously wrong — very serious charges that bore no reasonable relation to the evidence, racist media coverage declaring them guilty before they were charged and which continued after they were charged, at the committal hearing and again at the time of the trial, the police hype bordering on hysteria, at every court appearance. All these things were obviously geared towards the end result of a jury conviction. But in the beginning we didn't see them as linked. Then we began to see the links and how they all fitted into a pattern. The media coverage was based on leaks from the police. The police were issuing information which was not true, and the media was taking it up and embellishing it.

'The security at court appearances seemed no accident either. It costs a lot of money and effort to put marksmen on roofs, police with sniffer dogs on the street and to send prisoners to court preceded by blaring sirens. But it all says very clearly that these are dangerous and guilty people who should be convicted. They all form part of a structural pattern designed to put pressure on a jury and which brings about miscarriages of justice. In the Winchester Three case, in spite of all the stage management, the evidence was so inadequate that Mr King himself had to intervene during the trial to tell the jury that people who exercised their right to silence were guilty. And even then the jury could not reach a unanimous verdict.

'Recognising the pattern is very important. If each case, as it becomes established as a miscarriage of justice, is only taken individually — and of course each case must be taken individually on its own merits — but if we don't see the pattern and how the miscarriage came about, we can't raise public awareness to the level which will ensure that more miscarriages of justice do not happen in the future. Also, only a few cases get taken up effectively, and many are lost or forgotten because the people involved are not in a position to develop an effective campaign. I have come to believe very strongly that while every miscarriage of justice must be fought on its merits, we must keep making the links and highlighting the structural pattern that creates miscarriages of justice. Otherwise, we leave the system that creates them to continue to operate.'

Mary Cullen also now feels it is very difficult to get serious and honest debate about these issues in Ireland. 'Many people who were really concerned about the various aspects of the Winchester case were reluctant to become involved because they were afraid of being labelled as "fellow-travellers" of the IRA. Other people said — and still say — that criticism of British justice is "anti-British" and gives support to the IRA.

'The same thing happens with debate about Northern Ireland. Anything less than seeing the IRA as the only villains of the piece is labelled by one school of thought as actual support for the IRA and as anti-British. Debate is polarised into support for good or for evil, and people are slotted into mutually exclusive points of views. This makes it almost impossible for people who don't see things in simplistic terms of good against evil to get a hearing. The assumption underlying this labelling is that the problem in the North is due solely to the IRA and that if the IRA could be stopped everything would be fine.

'One does not have to be a supporter of the IRA to see the fallacy of this assumption, and how acting on this analysis makes the problems more difficult to resolve. I now see the need for an open and honest debate about all the issues, with recognition of their complexity and with no one insisting on their own infallibility, as one of the most urgent and pressing for all of us in Ireland north and south.

'Learning all this made us aware that we also have a responsibility to be concerned about Irish justice. Our experience with British justice taught us that we should not be complacent about Ireland either. We are brought up to assume that all is well with our political, legal and justice systems and that the people out there who run them are doing everything properly. Now I believe that this is not good enough, that it is not even fair to the people who run the systems to leave all the responsibility to

117

them. The price of liberty seems indeed to be eternal vigilance on the part of the citizens. We must take care and watch and speak out if we see injustice. Insofar as we don't we are condoning and supporting any injustice that may happen.'

The fact that her son was released does not mean that Mary Cullen feels she can now forget about justice. The former Winchester Three Support Group in her home town of Maynooth has maintained its identity as a group concerned with miscarriage of justice and is now considering the future direction of its activity. 'Because I was put in a situation which made me think about things I hadn't thought about before, now that our three are free I feel a personal responsibility to try to use what we learned in some constructive way. I can only hope that I find that way and that I have the commitment to stick with it.'

Relationships between parents and their imprisoned offspring are not always easy, either in prison or when they are released. 'Single prisoners coming out experience far more problems,' said a social worker from the visitors' centre in Long Kesh and Maghaberry. 'They feel closer to the men in prison than to their mother, and they feel guilt for that.' An ex-prisoner who spoke to a NIACRO conference on prisoners' families said he felt that prison was putting pressure on his relationship with his parents. 'I was afraid my parents would be frozen in the old relationships,' he said. 'I was their nineteen year old son when I went in. They might expect me to be their nineteen year old son when I came out. I had time to think about my parents. I formed a far closer relationship with them.'

Prisoners develop various survival skills in prison, and they get used to spending long periods of time alone. Indeed, those who deal well with imprisonment learn to enjoy their own company. This can often be difficult for their families, especially parents, who think there's something wrong if they retreat to their room for long periods. Often they must learn to deal with the very different needs of the young man who has come back into their lives.

People who have been prisoners may prove to be a burden after they are released. Leaving aside the question of being a financial burden (and in many areas of the North unemployment is so normal that someone being unemployed is not questioned), their presence may attract unwelcome attention to the family home, especially if they retain some political involvement. One former republican prisoner who became involved in working for prisoners when he was released had extra security devices fitted to the family home. But it was only when he overheard his mother say to his young nieces and nephews, 'You know you can't leave that door open when your uncle is at home,' that he realised how much this was an imposition on a hitherto easy-going household. He moved into a flat.

During their years in prison many prisoners, especially the long-term ones, develop interests and ideas they didn't have when they went to jail, and this can impose a new barrier between them and their families and friends. One prisoner was released after fifteen years and his friends brought him for a night out full of everything they thought he would have missed most during his seventeen years inside. 'There was loud music and girls in miniskirts etc. It was really embarrassing. I didn't want to be there. Then I told my mother I wanted to go down the town and see a play that was on, and she looked at me and asked me if I'd gone mad.'

While parents, brothers, sisters and friends, as well as wives and children, are drawn into the experience of imprisonment, they do not all respond to this in the same way. Their response is governed, not primarily by their relationship with the prisoner, but by the attitude of their community to the imprisonment, and the assumptions they bring to that experience. The recent policy of the Northern Ireland Office in setting release dates for life sentenced prisoners and SOSPs and allowing them parole at home in summer and at Christmas again affect different prisoners in different ways. Those already inclined to leave their involvement behind them and concentrate on family life will have that inclination strengthened. However, those who remain happily integrated into their movement will not have this relationship weakened by parole or release on licence.

On the whole the parents of loyalist prisoners were bewildered and shocked by their son's involvement in illegal activity, and loved him in spite of it. They experienced the imprisonment as suffering for him and for the whole family, unalleviated by any process of political or civic education.

The sons of those I spoke to had all broken their links with their organisations, and were looking forward to a return to the comfort of family life, and this was what their families earnestly desired, though there might have been a self-selecting factor at work here. However, others who have worked in the area report quite a high level of disillusionment and religious conversion among loyalists. This is related to the more general crisis of identity among loyalists, discussed at more length below.

The parents of republican prisoners, even if not supporters of the republican movement, were able to understand their sons' motivation and sympathise with it to a greater or lesser extent. Sometimes the experience of having a son imprisoned changed their political outlook and activity considerably, like Lily. Although from a very different background, this also happened to Mary Cullen. The mother of one republican prisoner became involved in the Relatives' Action Committee in Belfast, and went on to become a Sinn Féin counsellor. She had not previously been politically involved. Such a transformation, however, was uncommon.

Chapter Five

The Children

In recent years there has been growing concern about the effect of imprisonment on the children of prisoners, many of whom spend their childhood and entire adolescence visiting a parent in prison. In his book *Children of Imprisoned Fathers* Roger Shaw identified a number of problems, ranging from failure to thrive, ill health and disturbed behaviour to truancy and lowered school performance. However, as the Reverend William Hughes pointed out, 'for over two decades the question of the well-being of prisoners' children has been identified by sociologists, but ignored by the "establishment".'

Last year Carol Horner of NIACRO began a study of the children of prisoners in Northern Ireland, starting with those serving short sentences or on remand. It should be remembered that three quarters of the prisoners in Northern Ireland are serving long sentences of four years and more, and a quarter of them are 'lifers'. She pointed out that existing research showed that willingness on the part of the prison authorities to recognise the rights of the child could have a positive effect on the overall state of the family relationships. Another crucial factor for the children was how the mother coped, and how well the parents could communicate what was happening to the children.

One of the first problems for the mother was what to tell the children. Of those surveyed by Horner, most equivocated, and rarely told the younger children the truth. These were 'ordinary' prisoners, except for those held on remand, and some of them had committed sexual offences, which were more difficult for the families to deal with. One mother told her eight-year-old: 'He's your daddy and we have to stick by him. She sort of said "that's fine" and she never really spoke about it again.' Another said: 'I couldn't tell the youngest children the truth. I told them he had got a job in the prison — painting the walls. But I knew they knew he wasn't.' Yet another said: 'It's just an everyday thing, especially where I live. They think their daddy's a hero and all, 'cos their daddy's in jail. You know the way they get on.'

Despite the separation most of the children were close to their father, and the family sought to preserve this relationship while he was in prison. One woman said her three year old loved going to the prison, and talked incessantly about his father. Another said: 'The children were very emotional after a visit — crying — especially the wee girl. I had to sit with them for a brave while when we got home, to get them sorted out.'

Some of them also had problems with discipline and the general behaviour of the children. For one woman the problem was so severe that she could not cope and had to put her two youngest children into care. Significantly, she began by saying, 'I had no one to turn to when he was lifted.' None of these families were of life-sentenced prisoners, and the majority of them were not political, so they are not representative of the Northern Ireland prison population. However, the NIACRO study has only begun and will continue with the families of 'lifers'. It will be completed in two years.

Another social worker working with prisoners noted that problems often arose when the children were teenagers. 'The boys often have identity problems. Should they follow in their father's footsteps? The mother fears they will end up like their father, in jail. The father often does too. Does this mean that what the father did was wrong? It involves a difficult adjustment.'

Again and again the impact of the imprisonment depends on the support of the extended family and the community. The extended family is strong, especially in working class communities in Northern Ireland and, where they rally round, the children will have surrogate fathers in their grandfathers, uncles and cousins. Even where there is no imprisonment it is common for children to go to their grandparents' house for lunch, for example, if it is nearer their school than their own home. If there is no stigma attached to the reason their father is in prison (and there is not in the nationalist areas and strongly loyalist areas), the burden of the imprisonment is lessened. For instance, the difficulty outlined in some of the academic research for a mother explaining to a child about the father's imprisonment for a sexual offence, and dealing with their response and the neighbours' reaction, does not arise for the children of political prisoners.

But they may face other pressures. In republican areas boys feel compelled to live up to the heroic image of their imprisoned father, and may end up in trouble as a result. 'There are cases where boys especially end up in anti-social activity of a sort,' said Tony Caffney of Sinn Féin. 'There is usually an amount of bravado, like joy-riding and smashing through a checkpoint, though they would be a minority. They feel they have something to live up to Their father is an IRA man, in Long Kesh, out fighting the British. They hear stories about their father, and they're often greatly exaggerated. This puts pressure on the parents again. They might also be in trouble in school, but even then they'd be very together.'

'There's also pressure on the kids to do well at school. Education is seen as a form of liberation by republicans. There's no employment in West Belfast anyway, but if they're educated it will stand by them; it can help them in some way at a later date.

'There's an emphasis on Irish culture and that in the families as well. A large number of the kids in the *Bunscoil* (*an Irish language nursery school in West Belfast*) are the children of people who were interned or sentenced, and the women take up Irish classes as well.'

Younger children suffer from the trauma of their father's arrest, though older ones may have seen it before and be able to comfort them. Lucy's husband was arrested in connection with IRA-related offences for the second time recently, and her four year old daughter is still very upset. 'She was badly affected by the raid. She had two pet rabbits out the back and they killed the rabbits as well as taking her father away. She's bed-wetting now and won't go to nursery school.'

Most of the children who spoke to me seemed happy, bright and well-adjusted. They had escaped many of the worst effects

123

noted in studies of prisoners' families. It was difficult to avoid the conclusion that this arose from their parents' attitude to the imprisonment and the offence which gave rise to it, and that of the broader community.

Political prisoners, and particularly republican prisoners, act out of a belief system which is at least understood by the community, if not always approved of. It can be explained to the children in terms they understand, and related to a wider view of the world. As the child grows up, more and more of the father's philosophy is expounded, and this in itself can be a factor in building a bond between parent and child.

Danielle

However, all this depends very much on the child's immediate environment. Danielle is nine, and her father is serving a life sentence in Britain for conspiracy to cause explosions. Only her teachers and her closest friends in school know about it.

Asked why she didn't tell everybody, she said: 'No one else has a daddy in prison. I'd be embarrassed. Well, two other girls have. One's a real snob. She goes around saying her daddy's in prison for trying to save Ireland. The other is OK. She doesn't.

'My close friends know, they know I don't want to talk about it. The teachers know. I say my daddy's working in England, I say he's an artist. He painted a picture of me walking in a forest.' Her father does a lot of painting in prison, and sends the paintings home. His wife Geraldine and children are very proud of them, and of his academic success in prison. 'My daddy's very smart,' Danielle interjected into her mother's conversation. She hardly remembers living with him. 'I was only a baby. I was only two when he was lifted.' Yet on visits she is uninhibited, according to her mother, crawling all over him and keeping him up to date with all her activities.

Her mother is quite happy about her decision not to tell her schoolmates where her father is, although her father was hurt at first. 'Can you picture her saying, "My daddy's in jail in England for blowing people up?" It's all right for him, he's in jail, in the same position as everyone else. But outside you don't know who

124

you're talking to. If someone said to me, "Someone belonging to me was blown up," I'd die. What do you say to someone like that?'

Sinéad

Sinéad, whose father Phil, from Derry, is serving his second sentence, has no problem about discussing this with her friends in school. She is sixteen. 'I was four when he was arrested the first time. I don't really remember it. There's just photos and things like that to remind me. I was ten when he got out, and twelve and a half when he went in the second time.

'I remember going to visit him the first time he was inside. There were other kids on the bus up from Derry. We used to sleep on the bus. At first I found the prison very frightening, but I got used to it. He was on the blanket at first, and when he came out I said, "He looks like God! He looks like God!" He wore the prison uniform for the visit (*wearing the prison uniform was one of the issues in the blanket protest*). I remember thinking, "Look at him, with the big beard."'

Like most of the children of prisoners, she gradually came to the knowledge of why he was there. 'At first I just knew the police lifted him, and that was all. I found out why listening to people talking. People ask me what he's in for, and I say, "political," and they say, "Oh," like that. In school I'd say, "I'm going up to see my daddy," and they say, "Oooh." (*She rolled her eyes*).

'When I moved to my new school I had a teacher whose husband was in the police, and she wouldn't take any interest in any of us whose daddies were in Sinn Féin. In the secondary school where I am now there's a few in my class whose daddies were inside. I take my friends up to see my daddy. They say, "He's wild nice." They don't treat me any differently.'

She missed her father very badly for the first year. 'When he was here we got very close. We'd go down the town, and go into a restaurant, and he'd say, "Don't tell Mammy." He'd help me with my homework. Mummy doesn't. I used to write to him and tell him about who I was going with and that at first, and he'd tell

125

my mummy. Now I tell my mummy anyway. Anything I want to tell my daddy now I tell my mummy.

'I have a friend who's always fighting with her daddy. She can't understand why I get on so well with mine.'

Like the children of a lot of political prisoners, education is a high priority. 'I haven't got to see him since September (*this was November*). I couldn't take time off school. I was doing my GCEs. He's doing GCEs too. He sends me out GCE books. He did sociology like me, and there's competition between us to see who'll do best. I write to him about my school results. He's always pushing me forward.

'I want to go to college, I want to leave the house, to leave this area, to go abroad. I'll study sociology, biology, maybe. He keeps telling me to get on with my studies, to go out occasionally. He says, "Don't you be getting married. I want to walk up the aisle when you get married." All the boyfriends I had I always told them my father's in jail, and they say, "OK".'

The fact that her mother has effectively brought Sinéad and her sister up alone has also affected their relationships. 'We're not like mother and daughter. We're more like friends. One of my friends can't believe I tell her about going out with boys and that.'

Despite the closeness of the relationship, she does not necessarily agree with her father's politics. 'I do politics in school now. I'm learning about Conservatives and Labour and that. People expect you to vote Sinn Féin, but I might vote Labour or Alliance.

'My friends don't want the Brits here. But we don't want the killing either. It's not like the 1970s, when people were all for action. We think it can be solved by talking.'

She has at least two and a half years of memories of her father in the house. Her sister Gráinne was not even born when he was arrested. However, her mother, Dolores, is working at building an equally close relationship between her and her father. 'We talk about him; otherwise she'd forget him. At the beginning we had to lead her in to see him. Now she walks in to him and kisses and hugs him,' she said.

Patrick

Patrick is now nineteen. He was only one and a half when his father was arrested and sentenced to life imprisonment in Britain. He only remembers ever seeing his father in prison. 'I was always looking forward to the visits. I always used to jump into his arms when I saw him. When I was younger and I was leaving the prison it always used to break my heart, so it did. It was the same for Róisín (*his younger sister*, born six weeks after their father was jailed).

'In school another wee lad's daddy was in jail and knew me daddy. I used to say he was in jail for robbing a sweet shop. I thought that at first.' His mother added: 'I used to say he was working in England at first. Jail's an awful thing for a small child, something they see on TV that bad people go into. I remember Róisín came in one time crying because a child said to her. "You have no daddy." I gave her a photo of him to take into school.'

'When I was ten or eleven I found out what he was in for,' continued Patrick. 'One out of every nine or ten families had someone in jail. But they were different. They were mostly in jail in Northern Ireland. I didn't feel strange about him being in jail. It was just he was in England.

'In the visits we'd talk about school, about the troubles, about what was happening in the flats here. He wrote to us all the time. He never wrote about what was happening to him. He was always asking us questions about ourselves. When I started going out with girls I talked to him about it.' Asked if he sought his father's advice, he was indignant. 'He didn't need to give me advice. I'd give him advice! He thinks he's God's gift. He looks it too! He says to me, "When you go out don't be getting full, just have a few, and do what your mammy tells you."' His mother added: 'I never had an hour's trouble with them 'uns.'

Patrick has been going alone to visit his father since he was seventeen, and now brings his steady girlfriend. His father's imprisonment is just a part of his normal life.

127

Carol's Children

The idealisation of the imprisoned parent may be difficult to keep up once he is released. Carol has four children, the youngest born after her husband was jailed for an offence arising out of his involvement in a loyalist organisation. He served fourteen years of a life sentence, so the children grew up without him. He has been released for just over a year.

'It took the kids time to adjust,' said Carol. 'They couldn't understand that Richard was not perfect, that he wasn't the idealised daddy they expected from the visits. They thought that when he came home everything would change for the better for them, but things don't change that much.

'My children adored and idealised him when he was inside. He always talked directly to them, and had sweets for them when they went up. I brought them up to see him separately so each had his attention for that visit. He always remembered what kind of music they liked, who their pop stars were. He made things and drew pictures for them. When he came home they didn't get his undivided attention; they were pushed out of the limelight. For the first few months it was very hard, but it's settled down now. Teenage kids can adapt very easily.

'It's hard for him too. He's been in a world of men all these years, and he's asking why the children are like that. I say they're going through adolescence. I went through it already with two of them. Prison life is completely different to home life. They all help one another there, and they're disciplined as well. At home they only support you when they want to. It's more easygoing. Everything is in its place in prison. At home things are left lying around.'

Unlike many of the children in British studies, Carol's children coped well with the imprisonment. 'My youngest would say her daddy went away because she was born. And there were a few problems with my son when we moved and he went to a new school. There were a lot of essays about what the daddies did at work, with the car, at home, etc. My son felt he couldn't be part of that, and he closed up in himself. There weren't many one-parent families then. By the time the girls went to school there were a lot more. I told the school and they were very supportive, and from then on he did well. After that anything his father did, like wood carving or that, was brought up to the school and displayed as the work of one of the parents. I was a youth worker, and they were involved in that with me, so there were always a lot of young people around.

'A lot of wives put a brave face on it. It's not until you face it through a group or something like that that you realise you did suffer. You were discriminated against in a lot of things, like hire purchase, and with the DHSS, which does not classify prisoners' wives as one-parent families, so if you work you don't get the one-parent family allowance. When Richard came back a lot of the neighbours who thought I was divorced thought I had remarried, or that we had reunited.'

Explaining about a prison sentence to young children is difficult. 'I didn't tell the children where he was until they were old enough to understand what it was all about. Under the age of eight, children can't see time; time doesn't mean anything to them.'

Like many life-sentenced prisoners, Richard was 'knocked back' when it came to his review. 'He was knocked back for two years. It devastated them. Two years seems very long to them. When the two years were up they started to get very anxious. Once we knew the release date they were all plans.

'Then we couldn't carry out a lot of them, because it took Richard time to adjust and he couldn't do all those things. You don't really notice all their nervousness and apprehension until you notice it's gone and they're more relaxed.

'But you can never make up those years. My eldest son is home from college for a few weeks at the moment, and he was talking about his friends and that, and directing all that to me, although his father was there in the room. He had photos, and he took them out and showed them to me, and then was putting them back in the packet when I asked him, "Are you not going to show them to your father?" His father was away for fourteen years, and our son was eighteen when he came out. You can't make it up.'

Yet it seems that the children of long-term prisoners convicted of crimes arising out of the 'troubles' actually cope better with imprisonment than the children of short-term prisoners, both in Britain and Northern Ireland, most of whom were convicted of 'ordinary' crimes, though of course there are exceptions in both directions. It would certainly be wrong to extrapolate from the studies of the effects of imprisonment on children, which are based on short-term prisoners in the main, a view that the children of long-term prisoners would be worse affected.

'I think this is because they are victims of circumstances, of the troubles; they would never have been in jail otherwise,' said Carol. 'Especially in the 1970s, everyone was supporting them, because they were fighting for a cause. There's not as much community support now. A lot of families are breaking away from it and settling down.'

Community support is the key. Where the children feel their father is in prison for something not regarded as dishonourable by the community — and this is the case in the republican areas, if increasingly less so in the loyalist ones — there is no sense of stigma and the family is not isolated from the community. Combined, as this often is, with a supportive extended family, the burden on the mother can be reduced, though it is never other than heavy. There is also a burden for the children to bear, though this often means they seem to grow up early and take on responsibility to help their mother. Others, of course, react badly and express their anger and disorientation in anti-social behaviour. Whatever their reaction, it is unlikely that the experience of some tens of thousands of children whose parents have served long sentences in prison as a result of the Northern troubles has left them enamoured of the authorities they see as responsible.

Chapter Six

Loyalists and Republicans

As the discussions continue on the future of Northern Ireland scant space is given to the question of prisoners and their families and the context from which they spring — the existence of a situation in that state which has made armed resistance to it, and armed activity within it, the norm for a large section of its population. While there is much talk about violence and the need to end it, there is much less about the motives of those engaged in what is described as 'the violence' (a term always applied to organisations like the IRA, and not to any violence on the part of the state forces which oppose them). Indeed, part of ending 'the violence' seems to be the denial that there can be any rationale for it at all, and the exclusion of those engaged in it from any way of presenting their views. The best they can hope for is to be included in the musings of commentators.

Most commentators on Northern Ireland tend to present what they call the 'paramilitaries' as a homogeneous bloc, or as twin expressions of an identical phenomenon. Thus the 'paramilitaries' are a disease, and the activity of 'constitutional politicians' is the cure. The possibility of those involved in military activity having anything to say — other than when they are giving it up — is excluded. However, talking to prisoners from both sides, and to their families, shows that they do have something to say about the circumstances they found themselves in. It also reveals startling resemblances between prisoners from both sides, and equally striking differences.

The first thing one notices is the very ordinariness of the families in both community and of the young men who go to prison, convicted of what in normal circumstances would be regarded as terrible crimes. The only conclusion one can draw is that these are not normal circumstances. Indeed, in a BBC programme on prisoners filmed in Long Kesh, this point was made again and again by those interviewed. Eamonn McDermott from Derry put it most succinctly: 'We're normal people in an abnormal situation.'

Trouble with the law, going to court, dealing with lawyers, visiting prisons, were totally foreign to the overwhelming majority of the families I talked to, although they experienced poverty and unemployment, normally associated with crime. Their concerns were with everyday life, with relationships with parents, boyfriends and girlfriends, husbands and wives, with setting up and maintaining a home, with ensuring a better future for their children. But their perception of seeing what they knew and cherished under attack, or of seeing a better future for them and their children blocked by the political system, and having no avenue within that system to deal with either of these perceptions, drove them to take up arms and attack what they saw as the enemy. In doing so they were acting on the perceptions of a wide section of their communities.

Yet it would be a mistake to see republican and loyalist organisations as mirror images of each other. The circumstances from which they spring differ profoundly, even if they are two sides of the same historical coin. Their visions of history and of the future differ equally deeply. And this is reflected in the way in which they cope with what imprisonment and its aftermath (and, of course, violent death) bring.

'Loyalists have a huge identity problem,' said a social worker who worked with the family centres in Long Kesh and Maghaberry. 'They feel the paramilitaries came into being because the Provisionals were in danger of winning and the British would have given in. They feel it was up to them that they did not win, and now they think that Britain has no intention of staying here, and would negotiate with the Provisionals, so who are they fighting?' This sense of disorientation as they oppose the state to which they profess loyalty is expressed in many ways.

Republicans, on the other hand, see themselves within a multiplicity of contexts. They are part of the armed current within the Irish nationalist tradition stretching back at least two centuries, and which included the experience of imprisonment in every generation; they see themselves as part of the Irish nation from which they have been cut off by a border of relatively recent vintage, which was regarded with odium by all Irish nationalist politicians until the very recent past. Over the last twenty years they have also seen parallels between themselves and other nationalist and liberation movements fighting discrimination and foreign domination. Set-backs can be placed in the context of a long and chequered history of nationalist struggle, not as harbingers of the abyss of abandonment.

This can be seen in the magazine for republican prisoners, *The Captive Voice (An Glór Gafa)*, which publishes political articles, short stories, poems and news about the prisoners in various prisons. An editorial in one of the first issues says: 'For some . . . struggle is seen only in terms of direct militant action which attacks the most overt manifestations of oppression, such as the armies of the state . . . One of the aims of *An Glór Gafa* is to challenge this exclusive view of struggle, and its pages have given a brief insight into the extent and type of struggle facing Irish people daily; struggles against the oppression of women, against cultural oppression, against the destruction of the environment.'

The ideology of republicanism is thus quite sophisticated, and is combined with social and economic policies, albeit sketchy in some areas, which seek the advancement of the people they represent and address their dispossession and oppression. They and their supporters look back to the bad old days of high unemployment, systematic discrimination and appalling housing, combined with utter powerlessness, and determine that nothing could be worse than that, that there is no going back. Even if many of the social and economic problems are still there, at least now their voices are heard — albeit often accompanied by the sound of gunfire.

The loyalists do not look back to hopelessness, and do not feel that some kind of hope has been snatched from the present situation. On the contrary they look to the past with nostalgia and complacency, and to the future with dread. Yet the past complacency was always tinged with a fear that their situation was transitory and could be threatened by those whose dispossession they sensed rather than understood. Much of their sense of identity was born of the feeling that there were people much worse off than themselves, that they were better than the 'other' against whom they defined themselves. They believed that their relative security was bound up with the repression of those who had been dispossessed, and the rituals of Orangeism — its celebration of military victories against the natives, the invocation of divine blessing on their civilising mission, the proclamations of loyalty to the most enduring symbol of the colonial power, its monarchy, and the power of the symbol of closing the gates of a fortified city against the natives — all bear witness to the insecurity of their identity.

Republicans' sense of identity is fulfilled in the taking up of arms in pursuit of the national ideal against the army of the British state and its local allies; loyalists' sense of identity is fractured by taking a similar course.

And so those who do this often face an identity crisis when they are imprisoned, and when they come out their organisations, which do not have well-developed political structures, have little to offer them. The loyalist politicians who articulate their feelings and fears, like Ian Paisley, publicly distance themselves from the paramilitaries and seem indifferent to the plight of the prisoners and their families. Loyalist prisoners see in Sinn Féin people involved in politics who articulate the views of the IRA and identify with their prisoners. One of the most surprising things I found in the course of researching this book was the sense of envy felt by loyalist prisoners for their republican rivals.

This disorientation is compounded by a sense of outrage when the tactics used by the police and army against the IRA is used against them the loyalists, as in officially-denied attempts to pressurise people into becoming informers. The magazine *Justice for All*, published by a group of the same name on the Shankill Road, carries front page articles entitled 'Shoot to Kill' and 'Political Hostages', adopting the language of the republican movement. In its July 1990 issue it alleged that two loyalists who had just shot a catholic in the Ardoyne area of Belfast were themselves shot by the British army, in the context of suspected leaks about IRA suspects from the RUC to loyalists. In its editorial the magazine states: '. . . for many years Loyalists were muzzled through fear of being called traitors and suffered their injustices in silence. Through our magazine we hope to highlight injustices in general and to increase awareness throughout the world that injustice knows neither religion nor politics.' The editor of the magazine, William Smith, told me: 'There's nothing for people to fit into; there's no system.' The magazine carries articles alleging a 'Shoot to kill' policy against loyalists and alleging attempts to force youngsters from the loyalist community to become informers.

Alan is a former loyalist prisoner whose views have undergone great change through his experience of imprisonment. Now in his early thirties, he is a tall, intense man with short, blond hair, regular features and steady blue eyes. Like many ex-prisoners I spoke to, he talks easily about deep feelings and intimate thoughts, and is very articulate.

He was jailed when he was seventeen for an unlimited sentence 'On the Secretary of State's Pleasure' for killing a catholic, and was released last year on licence (he can be sent back if seen to be continuing with his old associations), after spending half his life in jail. He feels very vulnerable, not least because he was already on a 'working out' scheme (preparatory to release on licence) three years ago and was sent back.

'I was due for licence in February 1987. Two weeks before, the police came to the door at five in the morning and took me to Gough barracks and held me for two days. They didn't question me about any incidents, and I wouldn't talk to them. Then they offered me a blank cheque to get involved in the paramilitaries again and feed information to them. I would not do it. My licence was put back, they said I was "associating". I was only seventeen when I went in. The only people I know are people I knew in the paramilitaries.' His social worker and various politicians contacted the Northern Ireland Office and the RUC about his allegations, but both denied any knowledge of them.

'I was threatened by the police that the Provisional IRA would think I was active again, (*the implication being that they could assassinate him*) or I would be put back to prison. I was called back three days after I made a statement about what had happened to my solicitor and a JP (*Justice of the Peace*).'

It is unlikely Alan would ever have been in jail but for the present Troubles. 'My family is not political at all. They were very shocked. They are Scottish. My father was in the British army. They would look on themselves as British and protestant. They're religious, more so now than before because of what they went through. I don't think my mother really believed at the start it was I did it.' Like many loyalists who took up arms, he sees a specific incident or experience acting as a catalyst. 'There was a UDR man shot dead locally (*he lives in a country town*), and his daughter of thirteen had been shot in the legs. I went to the funeral. On the day of the funeral they brought the coffin out into the garden, and she was there in a wheelchair screaming for her daddy to come back. I was there crying my eyes out. I was thirteen or fourteen. There was a sense of revenge even then. I felt that then.

'I started to grow up with the idea that catholics were out to kill protestants, a sense of what you'd call tribalism, clannishness. Up until I went to the tech' when I was fourteen I hadn't come into contact with catholics.

'The 1970s were really bad around here. The town was blown up and there was rioting on a nightly basis. There was an awful sense of us and them in the town, to show who controlled the town, whose town it was. I had a sense of identity then. I don't really have it now. I'm still looking for it.'

That sense of identity led Alan into the UVF and soon into prison, and carried him through the first years of his sentence. 'I was in Crumlin Road on remand for six months. For people from the country it meant that their families had to get buses and trains. It was difficult financially too, with the food parcels. My mother often said she felt guilty if she didn't make them up. I didn't think about that at the start. You get very selfish in prison, and at seventeen you don't think about bills and stuff like that. If there's money you think it's just for you.'

He spent the rest of his remand in the UVF compound of Long Kesh with men from his own age up to about thirty. 'When

I was convicted I didn't really understand what my parents were going through. At the time most of us were not depressed or anything like that. It was an exciting time. At that time we were thinking, "Twenty years, so what? You'll be still young when you get out." At that time you thought you could do anything. I don't think that my parents understood that's how I was thinking, but because of it I was in good form. They thought I was bearing up well.

'For the first five years in prison I was on a high. The comradeship and sense of belonging was a good feeling. You can feel things from other human beings you're living close to without saying anything. I miss it terribly. You can't recapture it out here. I had that closeness inside, but I missed out on developing a close relationship with my parents. Now I can talk more about personal things to people outside the family than to my mother. It hurts her. Growing up in my family there was a lot of love but not much communication.'

He described how self-contained the world of the prison could become. 'I used to write to girls who would come and visit. Whenever I was writing to a girl I would sit waiting on them writing back. If I didn't hear within a few days I would wonder why. One time when I was in the blocks we cut the visits right down, and we stopped writing. After a week or so it was great; you didn't sit waiting on letters and worrying if you didn't get one. It was very easy to slip into that.

'After five years or so I started to mature, to think for myself. When you're inside for so long you run out of things to talk about; you start to read a lot. Those who can't read go to remedial classes. Reading is something to look forward to, a reason to get up every day.

'At first I read fiction, history, biography, current affairs, things that open your eyes. I read about the Christians in the Soviet Union and all that, I could identify with them.

'Sometimes the reading made me feel confused. For example, on South Africa, it made me feel sympathy for the black people. I used to think about them as niggers and I started to see them as people. It was the same with the Palestinians. I used to be 110 per cent pro-Israeli, and I went there when I came out. Most of

137

the Israelis I met were very arrogant, and most of the Arabs were old women in the street who were very friendly and would give you fruit and things. Though I know it is not as simple as that. But I saw the PLO was capable of crying, of feeling pain. It's the same with the IRA. It had never entered my head they were emotional people, like us. It was unsettling really. I also learned that there really were a lot of things wrong here before the troubles. I remember realising that if I was born a catholic I'd probably be in the IRA. It was very hard to think that. I couldn't say that to most of my friends.

'I couldn't discuss a lot of my reading. I knew something was happening inside my head, but I found very few I could sit down and have a discussion or a debate with without meeting blind prejudice, like on the South Africans. Even today there are a lot of beliefs and feelings and thoughts I have that I can't discuss with my friends. It would isolate me and even create hostility. My girlfriend is not politically-minded.

'I find myself lost at the moment. It has affected my mood and temper. One day I'd be so on edge I'd blow up over the slightest thing; other days I'd be so calm nothing would rattle me. There's a battleground in my mind and heart and soul.'

Many loyalist prisoners and ex-prisoners find a solution to their sense of dislocation in religion, but it did not offer a long-term solution to Alan. 'I always believed that because I was a protestant, at the end of the day I would be all right with God no matter what. Now I find the deeper you go into the teachings of Christianity the more troubled you get in your mind. I have a terrible problem with religion at a personal level. I'm trying to understand God without any preconceived ideas, and it is hard to come to God without any prejudice.

'I was special category and I left and went into the H-Blocks about 1980-1981. I was bored. Life had become very stagnant. I felt my mind wanting to develop. I felt I was going through a religious experience. I felt that in order to prove to myself and to God that I was sincere I had to relinquish special category. Also I needed a change. It was a hard decision; with the hunger strikes going on I didn't know what I was going into.

'I had an attitude of hope, that I would find myself. I was able to share this with one man who is now studying to be a minister, and who went through a similar experience. I was not looking for religion as an easy way for my conscience. Being religious in prison creates problems from the point of view of other prisoners and the staff.

'But I had a lot of problems in church, like saying prayers for the security forces. I know members of the security forces are responsible for murders and this created a confusion — does God say it's OK to commit a murder in a uniform? I have a constant battle with God. I come across people out here who say they have been Christians six or ten years and they say they have no problems with God. I can't understand it. They say you can't mix religion and politics. I feel you can; politics is part of human life. But I felt I was betraying part of myself if I was involved in religion. I felt I was living a lie.'

Nor does family life offer a haven. 'At the start I was on a high. I had no problems. Now I have a tough time at home. I like to be on my own a lot, to have time on my own and stand back and look at myself. I spend a lot of time in the spare room. At first my mother thought that was a problem. Now she understands that I need that space, but she doesn't understand the type of person I am. I can't talk to them about real, deep things.

'My mother is constantly worrying about me. Things might come on the news and I would just react; something happens and it goes into your brain and you don't have time to reason; it affects you emotionally. I have to battle through that in my mind to clear my mind of it. I have to work through it.'

Alan is more thoughtful than many of his friends, including people who were in prison with him, and that in itself is a barrier. 'For a lot of my friends, including people I did time with, life's a big laugh. Sometimes I wish I could be like them.

'People are afraid to let go of what they know. Especially from a protestant point of view no one wants their faith in the state to be shattered. I know people who don't believe a policeman can tell a lie. How do you start with people like that? I find it difficult to talk to people because they're not thinking for themselves. They don't understand who they are themselves, though they would fiercely deny that.

'It's hard to get to the truth of Northern Ireland because so many people are afraid to talk. A lot of paramilitaries talk as paramilitaries, not as human beings. These talks that are going on now, they pretend that the paramilitaries don't exist. They don't realise that the reason they are sitting down is because of the situation created by the paramilitaries. There is a big burden of suffering here which is being ignored. When you come from prison you're not afraid of authority; you speak your mind. I've been brought up at work for disrespect because I disagreed with a senior member of the staff. You're more sensitive to unfairness, to injustice, and because of your background you're seen as a trouble-maker.'

Alan desperately wants to bring the reality of what he sees happening in his community, and in his country, to the public eye. 'I would love to be involved in a play or something about Northern Ireland which would really show how it was. I've seen films about Northern Ireland and I've always come away disappointed. I feel there's a story to be told. My biggest regret is that at the time I was going through school I was only interested in the troubles.' Asked if he had considered trying to write a play or a novel himself, he explained that prison had made this difficult. 'When you are in prison the only thing you can have is your personal thought. That can't be censored or taken away. I'm afraid to write it down or let it go. Also from being in prison I'm reluctant to open up.

'The thing about republican prisoners is that they have Sinn Féin; they feel they can contribute if they want to; Loyalists can't. You have to rethink what you are. I'd like to get involved in something where I could talk openly and follow it up in some way.'

Eddie

Eddie was born and reared, and still lives, on the Shankill Road. He was also an SOSP prisoner, convicted at seventeen. He served thirteen and a half years. He received his 'licence' in 1988, which specifies that, although released, he can be brought back to prison at any time.

Like many loyalist parents, his were shocked by his conviction. 'My mother couldn't accept it. When she came to visit she would say, "You didn't do it, did you?" She was in tears every day, but the rest of the family would have borne it more than me. My father turned grey in a very short time. He had several heart attacks, then he broke his back in a fall, he got bowel cancer and now he's just had a stroke. My mother died on my first parole. I know all the stress affected their health.'

Prison was not a totally negative experience. He produced photographs, taken inside clandestinely, showing him and his friends posing in the sun in the compounds, drilling in UVF uniform, and one of about twenty around a table with mugs. 'We were drinking home-made poitín.' How did they make it? 'We got the recipe from the Provos.' Did they have much contact with the Provos? 'After a few years curiosity got the better of us, and we started talking to each other, swapping LPs and materials for woodwork and leatherwork. When the other side was playing football some of the officers would go to the wire and talk a bit. But the screws didn't like it; they'd send us back.'

He explained the difficulty loyalists had in dealing with the experience of opposing the authorities. 'Nationalists grow up challenging the establishment. Loyalists grow up accepting it. My father served in the RAF. I was in jail and I had an uncle in Parkhurst for explosives offences. My father got permission to visit him, and he was arrested off the ferry and served with a deportation order under the Prevention of Terrorism Act. He was never involved in anything in his life. He was very upset. An Englishman married to my aunt was deported back here at the same time.'

Prison did provide him with an opportunity to continue his education. 'Gusty Spence (*a former leader of the UVF*) was in charge when I went in, and he encouraged people to take exams and that. I did my O Levels, and there was a group doing the Open University who approached me to do it too. I felt I wouldn't be able to. Then I thought, what have I got to lose? I took maths and computing and eventually got a degree. The study brought about contact between us and the Stickies (*Official IRA*); we shared a study centre and ended up taking our tea-breaks together.

'I read a lot. I read a lot of books about the Red Indians, whose land was taken from them. And you never hear about what happened to the Aborigines.

'When I went in I wasn't politically aware. I just reacted to what was happening around me. There was pubs being blown up and people being shot in the area, and I thought I could do the same to those who were doing it. Then when I was arrested and went to jail the police and prison officers were all wearing the crown, and I thought, what am I doing here? I started to question the establishment. Some others did too, but some didn't.'

His experience has led him to sympathise with people like him in the catholic community. 'As soon as something happens the unionist and loyalist politicians want to do something hard against the catholic community, and that isolates them even more. If the police lift people for no apparent reason they give people a reason for their grievance. They can't turn to the RUC if there are problems in their area or they are seen as supplying information. When they vote for Sinn Féin people on the Shankill see it as 14,000 votes for attacks on them. But it's not like that. The loyalists are afraid.'

Of what? Of their way of life being threatened? 'In reality they don't have a way of life worth fighting for. They were told by the establishment that their way of life was being threatened by the nationalists, and they accepted what the politicians said without question. They were told that they were better off because they were loyal, and they believed it. When they were told the civil rights movement was a threat to them they believed it. Each time the republicans carry out an act of violence it endorses what the politicians say.'

Although he sees parallels between the experiences of imprisonment for both working class communities, Eddie is very critical of the republican movement for ignoring this. 'The republicans' international ideology is largely for international consumption. They don't do anything to attract the protestant working class. A lot of people on the Shankill despise Nelson Mandela because the IRA claim him and the ANC. I admire Nelson Mandela: he sacrificed twenty-seven years of his life for his beliefs, not for any action. He could have walked out years ago if he was prepared to give up his beliefs.

'Say on "shoot to kill," why don't they (*the republican movement*) ask how many protestants have been shot by the security forces. There's been a phenomenal amount of protestants shot dead on the Shankill Road, but the unionist politicians say nothing about it. Their attitude is that they shouldn't have been on the streets. Then the campaign of the republicans on plastic bullets was quite justified, but when Keith White was killed by a plastic bullet (in a demonstration against the Anglo-Irish Agreement on Easter Monday 1986), instead of using that to make contact with loyalists, they came across as gloating.'

Has anything positive come from this for the loyalist community? 'Just about every female in West and North Belfast would be affected by imprisonment, and it would spread into areas like Bangor and Donaghadee as well. Sharing their suffering going up on the buses they were bound together tighter as a community. They should be able to empathise with the other side as well, whether they do or not . . .'

Tony

Tony also went to prison as an SOSP prisoner at the age of seventeen. He served fifteen years before coming out two years ago. He differs from Eddie and Alan only in being from a nationalist background. 'My family was not political, They were affected by things that happened in the 1940s and 1950s, but in the 1960s there were all these new housing estates, and they moved out to Rathcoole. They had great aspirations; they thought you could get away from the problems of the past with a good education and hard work. They were at pains to make sure that we all stayed at grammar school.

'They had to revise everything when the family was burnt out in the early 1970s. In 1972 and 1973 everybody was talking about politics, no matter what age they were, including the kids at school. I would have been very careful not to express my views in the house. But it took my parents being burnt out to realise that not much had changed.'

Once in jail he too became part of the close-knit community there, and it deeply affected his personal and political development. 'It forces you to reflect; you reflect on a lot of things for a number of years,' said Tony. 'You also build up your ideas, you project, you think how things should be. It's often a bit of a culture shock when you get out. When you try to reintegrate into Sinn Féin it sometimes doesn't gel with the ideas you had.

'Education is a central part of this development. The majority would take part in formal education, and there's informal education in the wings which had far better attendance. The atmosphere was very conducive to creativity. You'd see people come out from Crumlin Road (*the remand prison*) and getting caught up in the atmosphere of the H-Blocks; you'd see their ideas being challenged. You had to really think your ideas through in there. You'd see them start writing, etc.'

Like many other prisoners, he misses aspects of imprisonment. 'I miss the strong feeling of community that was there. I miss some people who are still there. I really enjoy visits now. There's a big room with fifteen or twenty of the prisoners there, and you can go around talking to them all.

'You get very close to people; relationships are very open and very honest.' What happens when this attitude to relationships is applied to life outside? 'A lot get hurt. A lot of prisoners have very great difficulty distinguishing between sexual and emotional relationships outside.'

This does not just affect single prisoners trying to integrate into the social mores of the outside world, with the subterfuge and courtship rituals which make up the lubrication of social intercourse. Many marriages break up. 'People's whole circumstances change. Ten years inside jail isn't the same as ten years outside. The people change, and may not change in the same way. But having said that, some not only survive imprisonment. They thrive.'

Did they have much contact with loyalist prisoners? 'You would have met them coming to and from visits and that. To be honest, we didn't want to have that much dealings with them. There was something very authoritarian about the organisation, the OC (*Officer in Command*) would usually be the man who could fight in prison. It was very much a hard man thing.'

He responded to Eddie's criticism that the republican movement made no overtures to the protestant working class by saying: 'Any protestant who says he has more in common with the catholic working class than with the protestant middle class will be attacked now. I know of one ex-prisoner who did this on television and he was beaten up in his own area. If the constitutional issue is dealt with there won't be any more unionists and nationalists and this won't happen then. Then unity will be possible.'

However, he added that at the level of prisoners' rights and conditions there was contact and cooperation between loyalists and republicans.

'The comradeship of the prison is still there when you get out. We probably have a far greater network of support than the families have,' said Hugh, another former life-sentenced republican prisoner. 'Prisoners have certain values, like, whatever you have, you share with your comrades, your colleagues. You know they're not going to abuse it. There's not the same attachment to personal possessions that people have outside.

'Most of the people we would socialise with would be ex-prisoners. Even old friends who visited me while I was in prison, now they're into a really conventional way of life; they're all concerned about their careers, their houses, and that.' He was offered a teaching job when he came out, but opted for a less demanding job so that he could work with prisoners, especially those serving sentences in England.

Tony and Hugh are like Alan and Eddie in many ways. Like them they have spent about half their lives in prison, and are now in their thirties. Like them, Tony is from a working class background and became an SOSP prisoners while still a teenager. Hugh is from a more middle class background and trained to be a teacher, though he was arrested before he did much teaching. Neither are married, and both returned to their families on their release from prison in the past year.

They are also similar to Alan and Eddie in their obvious intelligence, in their concern for the state of the world, in the breadth of their reading and cultural interests, in their commitment to a cause, in their loyalty to the close relationships they built in prison. But they see no contradiction between the world view they developed in prison and their religious and cultural background, and have no difficulty in finding a way to express their views in legal activity outside the prison. Both are active in the prisoners' welfare department of Sinn Féin.

The vast majority of prisoners, loyalist and republican, come from the working class areas of the North, from the communities who have had negligible political representation since the foundation of the state. Although working class protestants voted for unionist politicians, these politicians did not, on the whole, come from their areas and did not share their experience. The same was true of the majority of nationalist politicians.

This has not changed since the beginning of the current troubles. What has changed is that the people concerned have found other ways of expressing themselves, outside the system and, indeed, outside the law. 'There is a sense here that the republican movement has given people a voice and it should be heard,' said Tony. Many of the prisoners have reflected deeply about their situation and want to use the experience of the last twenty years to ensure that things change for their community, though there is no agreement between republicans and loyalists on how this should happen.

A social worker who worked as a community worker in the Shankill Road and has worked with both loyalist and republican prisoners and their families for many years outlined the differences between them: 'The loyalists don't have the same vision as the republicans. They don't have anything to gain from this situation, but they want to minimise the loss.

'When the civil rights movement started first and they saw pictures of the houses in the catholic areas, a lot of people on the Shankill were shocked, because their own houses were worse. But instead of turning against the politicians who had lied to them, they blamed the catholics. Working-class protestants now know that they were used. But they have no equivalent to Sinn Féin; there is a vacuum there, there is no doubt about it. Some turn to religion and work it through that.

'All the discussion is about talking to Sinn Féin. The loyalists feel, "Why is no one talking to us? Should we step up the violence?" They see the republicans as having a more efficient machine and a better political voice. They fear they will lose. They feel vulnerable.'

She is critical of most public figures who appear not to want to hear voices from these areas. 'If you want to dismiss someone you say they're from Sinn Féin.'

However, she sees hope for the future in the prisoners themselves. 'Even the loyalist prisoners don't have the same difficulty as other loyalists in knocking the system and trying to work out some alternative. There is hope for our country and it lies, at least partly, in the lifers getting out.'

Chapter Seven

Beyond Prison

If up to 100,000 people have been affected by imprisonment in Northern Ireland, a state with a population of about a million and a half, it is to be expected that this will have an impact on the society as a whole. Yet this features so little in discussion of what is going on in that part of Ireland that an observer would be forgiven for thinking that it has no impact at all.

The majority of the people most affected by the troubles over the past twenty years are not those who make the political decisions, who do the negotiating with the powers that be. As Eddie, a former loyalist SOSP prisoner said, 'The people having the meetings come from a totally different background. They live away from the areas where the troubles are taking place. The people who make the decisions don't live in those communities. They don't know the stresses and everyday strains people have to put up with.'

So the years of impoverishment, of trekking to prisons, of coping with children alone as they grow up, of separation and grief, of children not really knowing one of their parents, go largely unreported. Where there have been miscarriages of justice these have gone ignored for many years until the tenacity of the families of those involved, and their few friends and allies, brought them to public attention. It is hard to escape the conclusion that women who are poor (in the main) find it difficult to draw attention to their problems.

In dealing with these problems they reveal great strengths and acquire considerable skills. But these skills are not automatically applied to the broader arena of the community. It is not possible to say that the working class communities of Northern Ireland have been transformed by the input of the women who have had to assume new roles as a result of the troubles.

The effect on the communities varies according to whether they are loyalist or republican. In the loyalist communities the impact cannot yet be fully defined. Many of the women who have had to carry the burden of the imprisonment of a member of their family still mainly apply this to their domestic situation, according to people working with them. 'It is down to the individuals,' according to Hester Dunne, of Justice for Lifers. 'There is a tug of war between what they feel they should do to help him get his identity back, and themselves. One woman said that all that running to prisons for fourteen years was almost forgotten; it was as if it never happened. You can push away painful experiences.'

Asked if this had an impact on the communities themselves, she said: 'Unfortunately no. I haven't found it so. When it's over they are trying to build a new life. It takes a lot of con-centration. Sometimes they start new families when they come out and the odd new baby comes along. The women have a lot on their plate if they're trying to get together with the guy again anyway. A lot of the former prisoners would be concentrating on domesticity and family life. That would not be a bad thing; the risk of reoffending would be less. Most of them are not out long enough yet to judge the full effects.'

A social worker working with prisoners and their families sees some transformation in the women from the loyalist community. 'Some of the women would have learned things and would apply them to their domestic lives. Say the man comes out and starts drinking again. A lot would say, "I know I can live without you. I know I can rear the kids on my own," which they would not have had the strength to do before.

'It has had more impact in the republican community, both on the prisoners and their families. The Provos are organised inside, with classes, etc, and they do things on the role of women and things like that. There's nothing comparable on the loyalist side, where if that kind of education happens it's on an individual basis.'

Tony Caffney of Sinn Féin's prisoners' department said that the impact on the women varies. 'Some become involved in the

Relatives' Action Committees; some become involved in broader issues. One women became involved in the Relatives' Action Committee, because her son was in jail, and she is now a Sinn Féin councillor.

'West Belfast is probably one of the best organised communities in Ireland as a whole. If you look beyond Sinn Féin to the different groups now involved in various campaigns, like the West Belfast parents and youth organisations, adult education groups, committees trying to do something about glue-sniffing and that, I'm hard pushed to think of one of them who has a strong male figure leading it. That's unusual in this type of society. Men would have been in charge of these groups fifteen years ago.

'Men now have no trouble recognising that. But they don't always recognise the importance of women's commitment. I know of one man who's practically an alcoholic now. His wife, who's a leading figure in the community, is the strong and articulate force in the family.'

In both communities the fact that women have learned to cope alone means that both they and the younger women who see them doing so in their areas now know that this is possible. At least at the level of personal relationships women are no longer seen as powerless and dependent. This must subtly change their expectations and their perception of their own capabilities.

But the broader political context is inescapable. Loyalist prisoners and their families have had to come to terms with the idea of opposing the state they passionately believed was theirs, and this has led to confusion and disarray. Most of them seek an answer, not in a coherent political outlook which would bind them together into an effective group, but in a renewed commitment to their families and domestic life, or in religion.

In a society where religion is closely bound up with identity, the evangelical form of Christianity which is popular among sections of the protestant population provides an ideology which allows its adherents to feel part of a community while not challenging the political *status quo*. It also explains the prisoner's previous action in terms of the influence of evil in the world.

Dealing with the problems of violence in Northern Ireland then becomes, not a political imperative demanding an examination of the past and possible criticisms of the state, but a religious one, demanding a contest with the forces of evil and a reliance on God.

This does not exclude women playing a role in the community, especially with regard to prisoners. Some of these groups have great concern for the prisoners and their families, and work to help them, and the women are important in this. One woman, the wife of a former life-sentenced prisoner, who is a member of an evangelical church which works with prisoners, said, 'It's behind us now, but you have to think of the people who you can help cope through it, so the years haven't been wasted.'

Although catholicism is part of the identity of the nationalist population, it does not play a major role in day-to-day life in the working class areas. Indeed, a priest has been seconded from St Peter's Cathedral in the Lower Falls to try to deal with the problem of non-observance in the community. While some of the prisoners' wives and mothers found comfort in religion, it played little part in the way most of them coped.

Because these women came from a community which had always felt excluded by the state, they were more prepared to confront it when faced with imprisonment. That experience could be fitted into a broader community experience. While the majority of those I spoke to were primarily concerned with their prisoner relative and with looking after their family, they maintained a general attitude of mistrust and hostility towards the authorities. Whether or not they supported Sinn Féin, their children shared that attitude.

Thus this experience of imprisonment became part of a generalised opposition to the authorities in Northern Ireland which is widespread in the nationalist working class areas, often uniting three generations. Some of the women expressed this by becoming involved in other activities, but even those who didn't become active are part of that section of the community which feels hostile to the political establishment in the North, and betrayed by that in the South.

Yet when groups from that community try to express their

views they are frequently accused of being supporters of violence. This obscures the questions they are trying to raise, which then rarely get discussed. The result is that the majority of people in the rest of Ireland, in Britain and elsewhere, remain ignorant of the day-to-day experiences of the people most affected by the only sustained armed conflict taking place in Europe. Surely listening to the people involved, and, in particular, to the women and children who bear the brunt of it, is the way to bring it to an end?

Select Bibliography

Hughes, William James, *The Effect of Life Imprisonment on Families*, MSc thesis, University of Ulster at Coleraine, 1989

Justice For All, Vols 1 and 2, 1990, Published from 252 Shankill Road, Belfast BT 13

Matthews, Jill, *Forgotten Victims: How Prison Affects the Family*, National Association for the Care and Resettlement of Offenders, London, 1983

Morris, Pauline, *Prisoners and their Families*, London: Allen and Unwin, 1965

NIACRO Information Unit, *The Transfer of Prisoners*, Report Belfast 1989

Northern Ireland Office, *Report on the Work of the Northern Ireland Prison Service, 1989-1990*

Rolston, Bill and Mike Tomlinson, eds., *The Expansion of European Prison Systems: Working Papers in European Criminology*, No 7, Belfast, 1986

Shaw, Roger, *Children of Imprisoned Fathers*, London: Hodder and Stoughton, 1987

The Captive Voice (An Glór Gafa), Vols 1 and 2, 1989 and 1990. Published by Republican Publications, 51-52 Falls Road, Belfast

Index

O

O Fiaich, Cardinal 87
O'Doherty, Shane Paul 33
Oireachtas Committee 114
Old Bailey 15, 78

P

Paddington Green 59, 70
Paisley, Ian 134
Paramilitaries 26, 61, 91-92,
  131-135, 140
Parkhurst prison 141
Parole 17, 34, 46, 68, 119, 141
Peirce, Gareth 33, 35-36, 63, 72
Power, Billy 15, 30, 81-82
Power, Breda 30, 80-85
Power, Nora 80-85
Prevention of Terrorism Act *see*
  PTA
Price sisters 32, 37, 112
Prisoners' Support Groups 23,
  106, 129
Prisonlink 99
Provisionals *see* IRA
Provos *see* IRA
PTA 18, 34, 36, 51, 54, 62-63,
  91, 115, 141

R

Relatives' Action Committees
  91, 106, 120, 150
Repatriation campaign 52
Richardson, Carole 15
Royal Commission 88

S

Secretary of State's Pleasure, on
  the *see* SOSP
Skuse, Dr Frank 74
SOSP 17-19, 36, 90, 107, 119,
  135, 140, 143, 145, 148
Special Branch 60
Spence, Gusty 141

Stagg, Frank 32-33
Stickies 141
Strip-searching 41, 67

T

Transfers 11, 29, 332-34, 36, 39,
  45-46, 49, 51-52, 55-56, 58,
  60-63, 68, 86-87, 89, 91, 106

U

Ulster Volunteer Force *see* UVF
UVF 18, 108, 136, 141

W

Wakefield prison 38-39, 66-67,
  72-73
Walker, John 15, 73-74, 112-
  113
Walker, Teresa 74-76
Walker, Veronica 74-76
Ward, Judith 28, 32, 85, 88
Winchester Three 116
Winchester Three Support Group
  118
Winson Green prison 73-74
World in Action 78, 83
Wormwood Scrubbs prison 68

Emily O'Reilly

Candidate: The Truth Behind The Presidential Campaign

> The definitive account of the most extraordinary election in the history of Irish politics
> ISBN 1 85594 021 3   £6.99

Nell McCafferty

Peggy Deery: A Derry Family at War

> Social biography at its best. Nell McCafferty traces the story of the northern Irish troubles and the way people have withstood the wars waged against them
> ISBN 0 946211   £4.95

Nell McCafferty

The Best of Nell: A Selection of Writings Over 14 Years

> Nell McCafferty is 'an original. She is one of those few lucky people who must be loved or hated, because she has a magnetic pull that polarises energy.'*Irish Press*
> ISBN 0 946211 06X   £4.99

Nell McCafferty

Goodnight Sisters: Selected Writings Vol 2

> More challenging and polemical insights into Irish life, politics and culture.
> ISBN 0 946211 361   £4.99

Mary Daly

Women and Poverty

> An examination of the extent of poverty and its impact on women's lives in Ireland
> ISBN 0 946211 620   £3.95

For a complete list of books Please contact Attic Press.